Natural Healing for
HORSES

Natural Healing for
HORSES

Jenny Morgan

Foreword by
Jan Agar Bergeron, VMD

STOREY
BOOKS

The mission of Storey Publishing is to serve our customers by publishing practical information that encourages personal independence in harmony with the environment.

Project editor: Cathy Meeus
Art editor: Hugh Schermuly
Designer: Nick Buzzard
Illustration: Richard Tibbitts
Special photography: Vincent Oliver
Proof-reading and index: Jane Parker
Production: Lyn Kirby, Kate Rogers, Sheila Smith
Direction: Patrick Nugent, Joss Pearson

Storey Publishing editor: Deborah Burns
Storey Publishing art director: Meredith Maker

Printed and bound in Dubai, by Oriental Press Ltd.

:10 9 8 7 6 5 4 3 2 1

Library of Congress Cataloging-in-Publication Data
Morgan, Jenny
        Natural healing for horses / by Jenny Morgan.
                p. cm.
        ISBN 1-58017-402-7 (alk. paper)
        1, Horses—Diseases—Alternative treatment. 2. Horses—Health. 3. Holistic veterinary medicine. I. Title.

SF951 .M85 2002
636.1'08955—dc21

                                        2001049514

Cover photographs: Bob Langrish (front left and bottom, back), Vincent Oliver (front right).

Contents

Foreword

When I was in private practice, I was often called out to treat horses for all sorts of injuries and ailments, and often these calls came at very inopportune times – such as the middle of the night. While driving home from these calls, I often reflected that many of the injuries and ailments I treated could have been prevented if the horse's owner had just used some plain old common sense. But I suppose the real issue was, and always will be, how do you teach someone common sense?

"Natural care" is virtually synonymous with "common sense," or perhaps it's the other way around. Regardless – as this book explains – the two seem to go together. Knowing something about the evolution of the horse and how horses live, eat, and behave in the wild will give you a basic understanding of what natural horse care is about.

Getting to know your horse is essential to providing the best care – you must know what is normal in order to recognize when something is wrong. Jenny Morgan tells you how to know your horse – what's normal and what's not. Most horse owners understand that the ideal environment for the horse is to be living free and wild, but if we are going to keep horses for riding, some confinement is necessary. If we must confine the horse, we must do it taking as much account of his instincts and physiological characteristics as possible. This book provides guidelines for doing that, from stabling to pasturing, to interaction with other horses.

Putting a bridle on a horse, a bit in his mouth, a saddle on his back, or riding him is not "natural" for the horse. For the domesticated horse it becomes a necessary evil. But again, common sense can prevail and these things can be done in a way that will minimize the negative effects. This book tells you how.

Once you have taken all the steps to make your horse's environment as natural as possible, and once you have come to know your horse, you must still know what to do if something goes wrong. This book provides a good overview of many common ailments of horses and tells you what "natural" remedies can be used for those ailments. But just as important, it tells you when you need to call the veterinarian, and it gives you some suggestions for working with your veterinarian to utilize natural therapies for the benefit of your horse's well-being. This book is a good first step in learning common sense (natural) horse care.

Jan Agar Bergeron, VMD
Editor-in-Chief
Journal of the American Holistic
Veterinary Medical Association

Introduction

It is hardly more than 5,000 years since humans domesticated the horse – a very short time in evolutionary terms. Yet we have expected him to come from being a wild creature, running free unfettered by saddle, bridle, or harness, into a docile creature who obeys our every wish and happily allows himself to be confined by the restrictions of bit and spur. What a huge expectation we have of him!

The ancestors of the modern horse

The first horse-type creature was *Hyracotherium*, formerly known as *Eohippus*, and also called the "dawn horse." This four-toed animal lived in the late Paleocene and early Eocene period, that is to say about 55 million years ago. This animal became extinct about 38 million years ago. A forest dweller, browsing on forest vegetation, he was not much bigger than the average dog. Around 36 million years ago the descendants of *Hyracotherium* began to move to the plains. It is possible that climate change, causing the retreat of the forests was one reason why this animal gradually became a grass-eating plains dweller.

When the horse moved to the plains, he became far more vulnerable to attack. He had to move further for his food and forage in open spaces. He needed extra speed to outrun predators and this meant longer and stronger legs. With his legs getting longer and stronger, he also needed a longer neck to graze. Changes in his teeth and skull also occurred as part of the adaptation to grazing. The number of toes reduced to three and then around 27 million years ago to one, enabling the horse to run even faster. The one-toed type is known as *Equus*, and all modern horses, donkeys, and zebras belong to this family.

Early horses roamed both the Old and the New Worlds. Indeed the main source of information about the evolution of the horse comes from evidence gleaned from fossil remains in North America. Early evidence was also found in Britain and in Europe. When the land bridge between Asia and North America sank below the sea some 10,000 years ago, the evolution of the horse in the Old and New Worlds became separate. Eventually horses died

out in the Americas. They were reintroduced to North and South America by the Spanish conquistadors in the 16th century. The chief American breeds therefore have a high proportion of Spanish blood.

The nature of the horse

Any animal living on the plains and needing to flee from predators requires quick responses. So the modern horse's senses of smell, hearing, and sight are acute. With almost all-round vision, he is able see a predator in sufficient time to escape. When you see a horse looking at something in the distance that is invisible to the human eye, and going into a panicky attempt to flee, he is acting on an instinctive response that goes back to his early origins and which was designed to save his life. Like many other grazers, the early horse became a herd dweller, adopting a social system that gives individuals greater protection from predators. In a herd system, the young horse also learns useful behaviour from older animals. For example, when a mare looks for healing plants when she is unwell, her foal will watch and learn.

Adaptations to grazing

As the horse moved to the plains, he developed the means to cope with a low-energy, high-fiber diet. In the forest he had access to an ample supply of

Running wild
The horse in its natural state is a herd animal. Constantly on the move, the herd roams over a wide home range, seeking out the best grazing. Any threat will provoke the whole herd to take flight.

Ancestral horse
Przewalski's Horse, a native of the Mongolian steppe, is considered by some authorities to be one of the oldest breeds of *Equus caballus* and the ancestor of modern Arab-type horses.

high-energy food and therefore needed to eat less of it. On the plains, where food was scarcer, he needed to consume much more of it to get the necessary nutrients – enough also to give him the extra energy to move greater distances to find good grazing. The horse became a forager, searching for his food with sensitive lips and then slicing it off with his strong front teeth. He would feed little and often, moving about a great deal at the same time. With this in mind, it is easy to understand why a horse or pony put into a field of lush grass gets into trouble. He is able to cut off the grass in far larger quantities than his digestive system, designed for poorer grazing, can cope with. The massive overload of nutrients obtained with minimum effort is bound to cause problems.

Horses and humans

Cave paintings from the earliest times show humans with horses. At this time they were probaby hunted for meat, only later being domesticated for use as a pack animal and later still for riding. Evidence of early domestication comes from Asia, from around 3000 BC. The first reference in writing that is thought to refer to a horse is from the Sumerian civilization of Ur in modern-day Iraq in about 2100 BC. The animal referred to is described as having "a flowing tail" and experts believe that this must be a horse. The ancient civilizations of Persia, Assyria, Greece, and Rome all used horses for war and work, and plenty of evidence in art and sculpture shows them being ridden and driven in harness. In the past 2,000 years the horse has worked for humans as a draft animal, a means of transport, whether ridden or driven, and a warrior.

Types and breeds

Over the centuries in different parts of the world, horses have evolved and have been selectively bred to suit the local conditions and the kind of work they were required to perform. Most modern breeds contain the blood of several older breeds. One of the world's oldest breeds is the Arab, whose fine-boned build is tough enough to withstand harsh desert conditions. In Britain, where the terrain is hilly and only short distances were traveled, ponies were bred for hardiness and stamina. Their small size meant that they could live on relatively small plots of land. This is typified by the Shetland pony, who was bred very small to live in harsh conditions on the relatively small islands off the north coast of Scotland. The English Thoroughbred, developed for hunting and racing, includes pony and Arab blood. Draft horses were developed from the early heavy war horses. This type of horse formed an essential part of the agricultural landscape until well into the 20th century.

The horse is an integral part of the story of the American West. Most American breeds are largely descended from the Spanish and English stock brought over by the early settlers. The cowboy most often rode the Quarter

From war to work
The heavy draft horse breeds that provided the power for transport and agriculture before the advent of the internal combustion engine were developed from the war horses of the medieval period.

Bred to win
The American Standardbred has been developed for speed, particularly in harness. Its conformation clearly shows its Thoroughbred and Arab antecedents.

Riding for pleasure
Today the majority of horses are kept for the joy and challenge of riding for its own sake.

Horse, a powerful, agile breed developed originally for racing. There are also cowboys in France, riding the native Camargue horses, and in Australia often riding the locally bred Waler. Some riding horses have been bred for their gait. Most famously, the Peruvian Paso, with its distinctive gait, in which the front and the hind leg on the same side move together, was favoured for its comfort over long distances. The Tennesse Walking Horse has a unique action in which the hind feet overstep the front, producing a gliding walk not known in any other breed.

Horses for leisure

It is really only in the 20th century that horses began to be kept in large numbers for leisure. At the beginning of the new millennium there are horses and ponies in fields and paddocks almost everywhere. Horses and ponies are bred in increasing numbers to serve this leisure industry. Horse shows, once only a minor part of agricultural and livestock festivals, are now separate events held over several days, attracting competitors from a wide area.

Changing patterns of horse care

In the past, because a working horse represented capital, he had to be looked after carefully and, because veterinary medicine was in its infancy, such care was more often than not based on natural remedies. The horseman really had to know his horses. There were remedies passed down from generation to generation for treating every imaginable condition. Some of these remedies would be seen as downright dangerous today, but some were wise and safe. Herbal medicine is one form of treatment that has come full circle. Used extensively in years gone by, it fell out of favour with the introduction of first sulphonamide drugs and then antibiotics. Now this therapy is enjoying a huge renaissance, especially with thinking owners who want to care for their horse's in a natural way that is free from unwanted side effects. Herbal medicine is seen to work and although it can never be a complete replacement for modern veterinary medicine, it has an established place in the horse-care repertoire.

The healing value of natural care

Keeping horses for leisure in the modern world often means his way of life has been pushed further and further away from the conditions for which evolution has designed him. He is stabled, often for hours in the day, preventing him from following his normal pattern of wandering about foraging, with the occasional burst of speed when a predator appears. If a threat is perceived and he is confined in the stable, what is he to do? This is where neurosis can appear and unwanted behaviours such as weaving, box-walking, and cribbing can start. Furthermore his feet may be softened by having shoes on them instead of being allowed to wear naturally. A bad farrier can put stresses and strains on the leg or even the whole body of the horse. While not being lame, the horse seems unwilling to co-operate or stiff and one sided.

A question of trust
A stabled horse is dependent on its owner to provide for its needs. His trust deserves to be repaid by the best possible care.

We should always be looking for ways to allow a horse in our care to express his natural behaviours. These include interaction with other horses, especially those that he knows well and are therefore part of his "herd." Freedom to roll and stretch his legs is vital. Getting muddy and dirty is important too – even if you have to clean him up afterward. Thinking about why he behaves how he does is important. It will help you to understand him and to work with him rather than against him. Leave his blankets off as soon as the weather is warm enough. Leave him out as much as possible. Feed him with good quality natural foods and the rewards will soon be obvious.

Problems of modern feeds
Possibly the least natural aspect of care of the modern horse is in his feed regime. If you look at the list of ingredients on any bag of compound feed, you will see many items that, while they may be safe for your horse to eat, are quite at odds with a natural diet. Your horse has no choice in what he eats; he has to eat what is put before him. Often the food is heavily disguised with molasses. His natural liking for sweet foods ensures that he eats the strange and unnatural foods we give him. Vitamins and minerals have to be added, because he cannot range freely and find these in his grazing. Often land is depleted of minerals by intensive farming methods in any case. Hay used to be cut from fields that had been naturally fertilized with manure. It was dried "loose" and then stacked in a haystack in which air could

circulate. Modern methods of harvesting hay mean that often with economic pressures, the hay has to be baled before it is thoroughly dry. The stalks of hay are tightly compressed into bales and these bales are stacked tightly together. In these conditions a variety of microorganisms are able to develop and these are inhaled by the horse when he eats, giving rise to respiratory diseases, which are rife today. The horse then may be given drugs – an unnatural treatment compounding a problem caused by unnatural care.

Repaying the debt

The horse has no choice about the situation in which he finds himself, which is often far from the ideal. Yet he continues to co-operate for the most part with our demands and desires. It is time for us to repay the debt that we owe him. It is time for us to appreciate our noble friend and to keep him in a way that he deserves, allowing him to express his true nature without undue interference or unnatural care regimes. By adopting care practices that respect his natural characteristics, from stabling and turn-out options, to feeding programs and riding techniques, as well as through the judicious use of natural remedies, you will be rewarded in the improved condition and behaviour of your horse and in the satisfaction you gain from knowing you are doing your best for him.

Natural spirit
Caring for your horse in a way that is in harmony with his natural instincts and physiology will allow him to reach his full potential in performance, health, and well-being.

TRADITIONAL WISDOM

Modern herbal medicine for horses has learned much from the practices of the Native Americans. They would have treated their valued horses in much the same way that they treated themselves – with plants, barks, and so on, that were found naturally in the areas in which they lived, mimicking the natural foraging habits of horses in the wild.

1

The Healthy Horse

*O*ne *of the fundamentals of natural horse care is to get to know your horse as well as you do any other member of your household. You can only know when something is wrong when you are familiar with the way your horse looks and acts when he is in good health.*

Know your horse

To get to know your horse, you have to spend time with him on a regular basis – ideally every day. This will help you to "tune in" to his moods, and if you do this, you will find him happier, more responsive and much more relaxed. If your horse is turned out, go to see him in the field at every opportunity, especially when you are not going to ride him. Have a little chat and pat him on the neck and then walk away. He will naturally want to follow you, so that when you do want to catch him, he will be more willing to come to you. Take time over everything that you do with him. In the high pace lifestyle that most of us seem to live these days, our horses are fitted in after work or at weekends. They may live in stables where most of the time they are looked after by someone with no emotional interest in them at all. Therefore the time that we spend with them is very precious. Make the most of it and you will reap enormous rewards.

Empathizing with your horse

Anyone who looks after a particular horse for any length of time will naturally begin to develop an empathy with that horse. You may just "feel" that he is off colour or upset without being able to put into words why you have this impression. Most of the time you will be right. You should aim to encourage and develop this "gut instinct" or empathy. It is also possible to cultivate a way of looking at and touching your horse that will help to tell you at once how he is feeling. When you practice the following examination and observations, making them part of your daily routine, you will soon reach a much greater understanding of how your horse functions.

First approaches

Before you first approach your horse and enter his territory, whether it be his field or his stable, let him get used to your presence for a few moments. You may alarm him if you, for example, suddenly appear at the stable door and walk straight in. Horses can feel very protective about their territory, even if they have not been there long. A horse that has been away from a stable for a year will still go back into the stall that he occupied when he was there last, and a horse that moved to a stable only the day before can part company with the rider some distance away and still gallop back unerringly to their new home.

Speak to him first: it does not matter what you say, but horses do seem to get to know various regularly spoken words and will gain much from your tone and inflection. Most horses know their name very well. Just watch him while he relaxes and becomes accustomed to your presence. Ideally he should be in a quiet place, either in field or stable, where he is free from distractions. Talk to him continuously in a low voice, observing him closely.

The gentle approach
A calm and unhurried attitude will help your horse to trust you and feel at ease in your presence.

Ears
Held forward and alert

Head and neck
Held up and centrally

Eyes
Bright and clear

Nostrils
Free from discharge

Mouth and lips
Relaxed and closed

Legs
Well muscled, squarely supporting
the body weight

General appearance

He should be standing evenly on all four feet with his tail relaxed and central
and his head held neither too high or very low. Look over his body and check
for signs of obvious tension in any particular place. His coat should be glossy
(see page 29), shining in sunlight even if it is dirty.

First touch

When you have finished your observations from a distance and you are sure
your horse is at ease with your presence – this may take only a few moments
for a horse that knows you well – you can touch him. Start with the neck.
The side of the neck is one of the least threatening places to touch him.
Stroke him along his neck and onto his body. Feel his skin for lumps and
bumps, and anything else that was not there before. After stroking all over

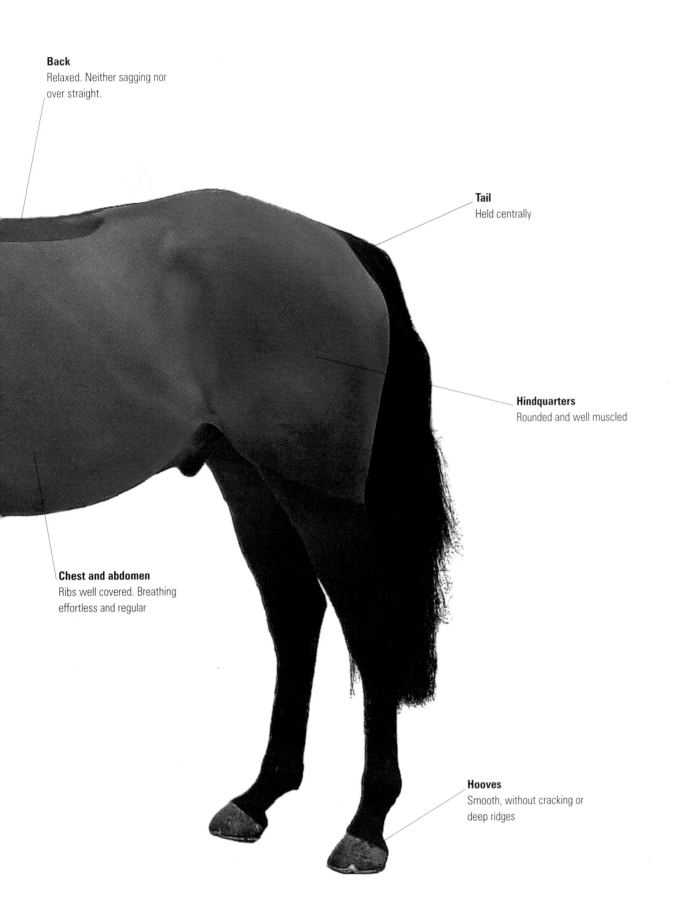

Back
Relaxed. Neither sagging nor over straight.

Tail
Held centrally

Hindquarters
Rounded and well muscled

Chest and abdomen
Ribs well covered. Breathing effortless and regular

Hooves
Smooth, without cracking or deep ridges

CHECKING FOR PROBLEMS

1 Start your regular examination from the front of the horse and stroke him all over using firm hand pressure. A touch that is too tentative may make your horse nervous. Use fingertip pressure along the spine from the poll to the base of the tail to feel for areas of tension, lumps, or other abnormalities.

2 With regular examination you will become familiar with your horse's anatomy and will quickly recognize a lump or swelling that is new. Watch your horse's reactions: he may let you know if a particular spot is tender or painful.

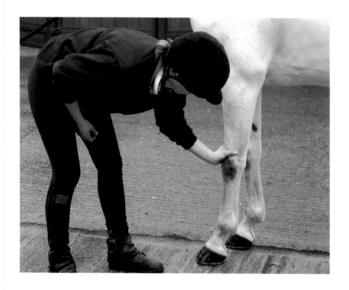

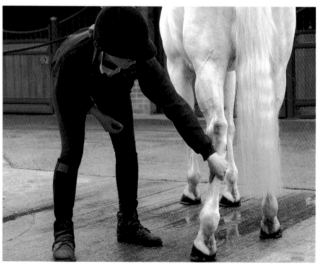

3 Starting from the top, cup your hand around the front of each leg in turn and, using firm pressure, work your way downward, feeling for any unusual lumps or bumps. Use your thumb to examine the normal indentations of muscles and bones of the horse's leg

4 Repeat the procedure down the backs of the legs. You will soon become familiar with the look and feel of your horse's limbs and will notice the presence of anything out of the ordinary. Consult your vet if you notice anything that concerns you during the course of your regular examination.

his body from poll to tail, go on to his legs. Be very thorough here, feeling for any areas of heat or tenderness. Horses have bony legs with various flat bits and protruding bits. Get to know what a normal leg should feel like. Most horses have the odd battle scar or two, whether an old wound scar or hardened splints (see page 137). Once you know what has always been there, you will quickly see any new problem. For further information on ways of stroking and feeling that will suit your horse, see the massage routine on page 73 and the information on Tellington Touch on page 189.

Head

Look next at his head and face. His expression should be calm and friendly. Stroke his forelock, unless he is head shy, in which case you should always approach from the side. Feel the front and sides of his face. Tooth problems can manifest themselves with heat and/or swelling on the face, so feel along the line of the teeth from the outside (see also below).

Nostrils and breathing

His nostrils should move very slightly as he breathes, but should not be flaring, red, or sore. Any discharge apart from a slight dampness in cold weather is a possible sign of ill health. His breathing should be regular and even, and completely quiet. At rest the average horse takes between 8 and 12 breaths per minute. If his breathing is laboured and his nostrils are flaring as he breathes, he may have a raised temperature (see page 116 for instructions on how to take your horse's temperature).

Ears and eyes

A horse's ears are a very good indicator of how he is feeling. At rest they will be either forward or relaxed, neither forward nor back. The horse puts his ears forward when he is concentrating or looking at something. He puts them back when he is unhappy or in pain. However, there are always exceptions to the rule. Some horses habitually stand with their ears back, but are in fact perfectly well and happy. This demonstrates the importance of getting to know the horse with which you are living and working. His eyes should be bright and clear and with no sign of discharge.

Teeth

It is vital that you monitor your horse's teeth carefully. A horse's teeth grow throughout life and are kept in trim by grinding on the opposite tooth. A regular dental check up should be part of any horse's health-care program.

Calm and alert
Your horse's expression tells you a lot about his overall well-being. A horse that appears to take a relaxed interest in his surroundings without signs of undue stress is likely to be in general good health.

This inspection should be carried out by a veterinarian or a qualified equine dentist about every 12 months.

Coat and skin

His coat should be glossy, but this does not mean it has to be show-ring clean. In winter an unclipped horse will have grease and dirt in the coat. This is normal and necessary for health. However, when there is some sunlight, you should be able to detect a sheen. The coat will be standing out nicely from the skin especially in cold weather, and should feel warm and dry (unless he has been out in the rain!) to touch. The skin should move easily over the bones and be free from rashes and unexplained dry or bald patches. The mane and tail similarly should be free from scaly or dry flakes, and should be of a reasonable thickness for the breed. Manes and tails vary a lot, for example, an Arab has a fine silky mane and tail, but a Shetland pony has thick, wiry hair. Both are normal. Check the coat for thorns and other foreign bodies among the hairs.

Clear eyes
Examine your horse's eyes regularly. They should be clear and bright. Discharge may be a sign of infection.

Muscle condition and weight

Condition on a horse is a subjective thing. A show jumper should carry much more weight than a racehorse. However, as a general rule, a horse is too fat if the crest of his neck is creasing in rolls when he puts his head up, or if his belly swings from side to side when he is moving. You should be able to feel the ribs but they should not be sticking through the coat. A horse is too thin when his bones show – that is to say his ribs and hip bones are clear to see. Being overweight is not desirable because the extra load places strain on the horse's joints and ligaments and, if he is ridden, on the heart and lungs. It is easy to cure by cutting down on food and increasing exercise. Being underweight when on a normal diet is always more serious, and may indicate ill health. It should be investigated by your vet.

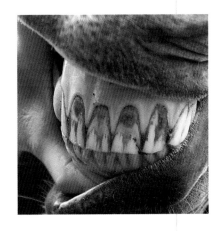

Healthy gums
Your horse's gums should be pink and firm. Areas of redness could indicate infection.

Hooves and feet

Good foot care is an important part of every horse's routine and this is your daily opportunity to check the condition of his hooves and of his shoes, if he wears them (see also Grooming routine, page 56). If the feet feel hot when

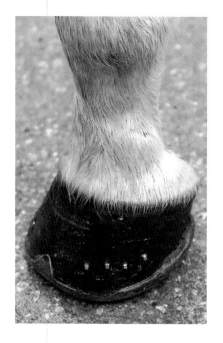

Hoof appearance
Well cared for feet, such as this newly shod hoof, are one the foundations of horse well-being.

you handle them, it may be the first signs of laminitis or there may be a foreign body in the hoof that has caused infection and inflammation. An unpleasant smell is usually a sign of a fungal infection of the frog or of another type of infection. Any foot problem requires have further investigation; the old saying, "no foot - no horse", is absolutely true.

Shod hooves should be examined to ascertain the state of the shoes. There should be no risen clenches (the ends of the nails that show through the foot about half way up) and the shoe should be firmly on the foot. The length of foot should be noted so that a check can be kept on when you might need the farrier. The coronet band should be clean and healthy. This is where the hoof grows from and any sign of damage should be either noted or shown to the vet depending on severity.

Droppings

Droppings vary according to diet but as a general rule they should be greenish brown in colour and passed in balls which vary in size according to the size of horse and which break on contact with the ground. Horses on grass all the time will have greener droppings that may not be so well formed. Any variation from the normal, which cannot be explained by being out at grass longer than usual or on medication or some other detectable phenomenon, should be reported to the vet.

Healthy sole
Don't forget to check the condition of the sole and frog. These should be free from redness or swelling.

Movement

A healthy horse is alert and has plenty of energy. But every horse is an individual and some show their high spirits more than others do. Some horses never go for a good gallop in the field and some make this their first job every morning. It is only when your horse changes from his usual pattern of behaviour that you should take notice.

See how he moves without a rider. He should use himself freely, moving on all four legs equally. You will soon know what to look for. In every pace, whether walking, trotting, cantering, or galloping he should show a natural rhythm. Whether he moves extravagantly or plainly is of no consequence – whatever is his normal way of moving is what is right for him and is the movement that you should be looking for.

Observing your horse

If you are handling a horse alone and cannot see him in the field – or if when you turn him out, he will only walk away, put his head down, and graze, then you will need help. You can lunge (longe) him, but it is not always possible to see exactly what is going on when he is working in a circle. The best method is to get someone else to lead him. Your helper should take him about 60 to 90 feet (20–30 m) away and trot him back towards you. They should take a line straight at you and you should move away only to let the horse go past and then take up a position behind him in a direct line as he continues for a similar distance.

For a horse to be truly "square" on his legs, a plumb line should pass through the knee, fetlock and the back of the hoof (or hock, fetlock, and back of hoof for the hind limb). However, this is not always the case and horses with even

Moving freely
If you are lucky enough to have a helper, you can make the most of the opportunity to watch how your horse moves while she leads him at the walk and trot.

LAMENESS INDICATORS

If you find it hard to detect lameness then take every opportunity to study any horse that is lame. This means looking at numerous horses as they trot and carefully examining the movements, looking for tell-tale signs of unevenness in the pattern of movement. Lameness can also be seen by the slight nodding of the head when the painful leg is put to the ground, although this may not always happen.

Lameness can take several forms and more explicit details of detecting lameness can be found in Chapter 6. However, the basic pointers are as follows:

- Not moving evenly on all four feet.

- Not standing evenly on all four feet, although a hind leg may be rested without it meaning a problem.

- Reluctance to move forward or to increase pace.

- Nodding head or favouring a leg in trot.

quite marked variations from the norm may be perfectly sound when trotting. The back leg should have the point of the hip and the front of the hoof roughly in line, but again this may well vary. For example, Arab horses often have long sloping pasterns, which would put the front edge of the hoof in front of a line from the point of the hip, yet Arab horses are among the most sound and hardy of mounts.

Tail carriage

In all paces his tail should be moving freely, too. If it is not held in the center or is clamped tightly down (except in very cold and/or wet weather) there may be a problem. A tail held high above the back when galloping around the field is just a sign of excitement.

Standing square
Look for vertical alignment of the knees of the front legs and fetlocks. In this photograph the near front leg is aligned. On the hind legs, look for vertical alignment of the point of the hip and the front of the hoof. The far hind leg of this horse achieves this alignment.

The unfamiliar horse

There will be times when you have to handle or assess an unfamiliar horse. This may be because you are looking at a new horse with a view to buying or because you are riding away from home. In all cases, it is important that you approach any horse you don't know (and who doesn't know you) in a quiet and sensitive way. If you are going to ride a new horse, do spend a little time just talking to him before you get on. Surely it is only polite to introduce yourself before you get on his back?

Initial assessment

If you are going to see a horse that you might buy, start your assessment by a general observation of his demeanour: just stand close to him and look at him carefully. Is he relaxed – or is he nervous of a stranger? If he accepts you readily he is probably a friendly and relaxed character. If he looks a little concerned but does not back away or put his ears back at you, then he is probably just not very used to strangers and may still be absolutely fine. If he backs off, pulls away from the handlers or puts his ears back at the very sight of you, you would be wise to think again.

Making a new friend
Always approach an unfamiliar horse with sensitivity and caution. Making first contact by stroking the neck is non-threatening. Speak to him softly and avoid sudden movements that may alarm him.

If all seems well, remembering to breathe deeply and slowly, approach him and hold out your hand. Body language is very important here. If you march up, staring him in the eye and thrust out your hand, he may well retreat, even if only a little. If you approach slowly with your head slightly bowed (in a submissive posture) and gently extend your hand, chances are that he will stand and allow you to stroke him. Never approach the face of strange horse. He will see this as a threat. The side of the neck or the shoulder is best for a first approach. After this proceed with the checks described on the previous pages.

Buying a new horse

When you buy a new horse, be sure that you like his personality as well as his looks and ability. You are going to have to live with this horse and if he has traits that you do not like when you go to see him, then you will like them even less when you have him home. It is imperative to spend as much time as possible with a horse before you buy him. If you can have him on trial, so much the better, but if you do this, do ensure that he is adequately insured.

Getting to know each other
Your decision to buy a particular horse should not be made in a hurry. A leisurely test ride is an important opportunity to discover his qualities and faults.

Questions to ask

As well as satisfying yourself that your prospective new horse is suitable for the job you have in mind, it is important to ask the present owners in detail about his medical history, and to make specific enquiries about his regular health maintenance program such as worming and dental checks. Make sure you get clear answers to the following questions :

- Is he easy to catch, load, shoe, clip, groom, and tack up?
- Does he get on well with other horses when turned out or being ridden in company?
- Is he prone to any health problems, such as laminitis or colic?
- Does he have any stable vices, including weaving, wind-sucking, cribbing, and box-walking?
- Is he reliable in traffic?
- Does he shy or bolt?
- Why is he being sold?
- What kind of work has he been used for?

A compatible character

It is very important that you choose a horse with whom you feel comfortable. For example, if you like everything about a horse but he is a wind-sucker (see Equine stereotype behaviours, page 108), do you have the temperament to cope with this problem? It can be extremely irritating when you are working in the stable to hear your horse swallowing air all the time or have him biting the door of the stable when you are trying to get his bridle on. If you are not relaxed about this habit, then you might find that the relationship between you deteriorates very quickly. Similarly, if you are a nervous or inexperienced rider, it will not work to invest in a high-powered type of horse and hope you will "grow into" him. He will probably just frighten you and put you off riding forever!

A gradual transition

It is worth bearing in mind that a horse that has been kept on a very artificial regime – for example, if he has been stabled most of the time and put onto a horsewalker for exercise when his owner does not ride – may take several weeks, if not months to adjust to a more natural regime. Horses are notoriously resistant to change and react badly when their routine or way of life is suddenly altered. Therefore you need to be prepared to wait for a few weeks until he has fully settled into his new environment and work routine before you make a final judgment on his suitability for your needs.

2

A Healthy
Environment

The horse's natural environment is one in which he is able to run free outside in a herd. However, for practical reasons most horse owners need to have their horse readily available to be ridden or worked, so we stable him for all or part of the time. If horses have to be kept in this way for our own convenience, then for their health and well-being, we must do all we can to make the stable a safe and comfortable place for them, taking account of their needs and instincts.

Learning from Nature

Living naturally in the wild in a herd, a horse always has equine company. The members of the herd each have their place in a strictly defined hierarchy, providing safety and security. Turned out either alone or with a bunch of unknown horses in a field, a horse is likely to feel isolated or insecure. In the wild the horse exercises regularly for relatively short periods throughout the day and night, instead of in a single long session once a day. For a horse in the wild the search for food is an overwhelming preoccupation, with the herd constantly moving on to new pastures. The combination of unceasing movement and a coat that is allowed to grow to its natural thickness, means that a horse can regulate his temperature throughout the day and through the changing seasons in a natural way. When planning an environment for a domesticated horse, we should never forget the kind of life he was designed to lead. Instead we should use our knowledge of his natural way of life to provide an environment that is sympathetic to his underlying nature and allows him to express his instinctive patterns of behaviour.

Where to keep your horse

The place in which you will keep your horse may be largely decided before you buy him. If you have land and buildings or stables at your home then this will probably be his home, too. If you do not have these facilities or live in a town, then a rented stable will be your only choice. When choosing a stable, bear in mind the principles of a natural environment and look for an establishment that offers the kind of facilities that will help you provide the best for your horse. For example, never choose a stable that has no facilities for turning out horses regularly. While the odd day indoors in very bad weather does no harm, most horses need to spend time in the field or paddock every day, even if stabled at night. However, the land used for the turn-out should be readily accessible to you or to someone else for observation at least twice a day, so that any problems can be identified and dealt with promptly.

A healthy stable

Even if you are adapting existing buildings as stables, incorporate as many of the suggestions for building new stables as possible into your plans. The first consideration is the siting of the stable. You should take into account the direction of the prevailing winter winds. Horses get much colder standing in a stable then they would, for example, standing under a hedge outdoors. Outdoors they would move about when they began to feel cold. Indoors they do not have that option. If a cold winter wind is blowing snow in through the top door onto them they will soon be very cold. Next consider the direction that the sun comes from in the middle of a summer day. Many horses like to come into their stable in the heat of the day to escape the flies and to have a quiet sleep in peace. This works especially well when they are able to graze in the field during the night. However, if the sun is shining in directly on them in the stable and again they have no way to escape, then heat stroke is a real possibility. The main stabling options are the barn system, popular in North America (see page 40), and the outside stable block, incorporating one or

A busy stable
The stable arrangement most common in Europe consists of loose boxes opening onto a central yard. Whatever method of stabling you choose, a well-maintained, ordered environment makes a significant contribution to your horse's health.

THE BARN SYSTEM

A barn system consists of a large building containing two rows of boxes facing each other with a wide passageway, up the center. With doors at each end it is very easy to build a wind tunnel if the center passageway is aligned to the direction of the prevailing wind. The advantages of this system are that the horses always have company; it is easier to work inside in bad weather; and the horses keep each other warmer than in individual stables. The disadvantages are that infections can spread more easily, it is more difficult to maintain adequate ventilation, which may encourage dust allergies; and smoke and/or flames are difficult to contain in the event of fire.

more loose boxes, usually with Dutch (divided) doors, facing into a yard, a design widely used in Europe. One of the advantages of this system is that of ventilation – each stable is open to the outside air. In addition, infections which can spread rapidly in a barn are more easily controlled. However, it is also harder to keep the horses warm in severe winter weather.

Air flow

Ventilation is absolutely vital in stables. It is important that a horse has constant fresh air, but this should not mean that he should be allowed to live in a draft. It is better to put a blanket on than to close doors and windows. Doors should be in two halves so that the top half can be left open except in very bad weather. In a barn a window at the back can also be left open. Ideally, fit windows that are hinged at the bottom so that when they are left open the air is directed up over the horses back. Plexiglas (perspex) is always a better choice than glass, and if this is not possible then a grid without glass is also acceptable providing that the window opening is high enough for the path of the air flow to be higher than the horse. There should also be some kind of ventilation in the roof. Stale warm air rises and collects in the roof space and this is not healthy.

Drainage and hygiene

Good drainage is essential for the health of your horse. Horse urine is remarkably strong smelling, and the ammonia fumes from poorly drained bedding can cause respiratory problems. If you are taking over an existing stable, you should also consider washing down the stable floor and walls. This should be done at regular intervals but special attention should be paid to a stable where a sick horse has been stabled.

Box size

Whatever type of stable building you use, you will need to make sure that your horse has enough room to take a few steps, turn, and lie down. The minimum space requirement for a horse is about 12 feet (3.5 m) square. A pony can manage with a little less, say 10 feet (3 m) square. A foaling box for a mare and foal needs to be at least 15 feet (4.5 m) square. Ensure that doorways are high enough for the size of horse; at least 3 feet (1 m) above his head as some horses throw their heads up when negotiating a doorway. Be sure that the doorway is wide enough for you and your horse. The minimum size of door for safety and ease of access for an average horse is 8¼ feet (2.5 m) high and 4 feet (1.2 m) wide. This can be a little less for small ponies.

Stalls, in which the horse is tethered in an area not much wider than he is, are not acceptable if you are aiming for natural horse care. The horse cannot move or lie down. They are really only suitable for horses to stand in for a short time, such as when ready for use in a riding school.

Preventing boredom

Many bad behaviours among stabled horses result from boredom. New stables should therefore be built keeping in mind the need to provide interest for the occupants. For example, a stable block built in a square around a central arena or paddock area allows the horses to watch other horses exercising and the normal activities of a busy stable. Similarly, two rows of stables facing each other are always more interesting for the horses than one long line. If you are building a barn system, then you might consider windows in the back of the stables so that the horses can see outside as well as the other horses inside.

Safety checks

On moving your horse to a new stable, you should first check all round that there are no nails or other projections on which he might injure himself. If there are fixtures such as a manger or water system, then the edges can be covered with

TIP

If your stables are already built and you find that you have weather problems, then this can be helped by fitting a top door and closing it in winter and by hanging shades (dark-coloured cotton sheeting works well) during summer.

TIP

Horses should always be tied to a short length of breakable string rather than directly to a fixed metal ring. If a horse is tied directly by a strong rope, which is possibly attached to a virtually unbreakable nylon halter and he panics, he can break his neck or at least do serious damage rather than break the halter or rope. This is also one reason why leather halters (headcollars) are always preferable. They are not usually stronger than the horse's neck.

Involved in the action
Most horses enjoy observing the activity in a busy stable or barn. Preventing boredom is one of the most important considerations for equine well-being.

BEDDING CHOICES

Straw	The most commonly used bedding material, straw is cheap and usually readily available. It provides a good soft bed and is relatively easy to keep clean. The disadvantages are that some horses will eat it. The dust it creates can also cause respiratory problems in sensitive horses. Straw is also somewhat bulky for disposal. **Cost category:** low.
Wood shavings	Easily available in polythene-wrapped bales. Shavings are better than straw for horses with respiratory allergies. Shavings are quick and easy to muck out and less bulky to dispose of than straw. This form of bedding also absorbs odours more effectively than straw. **Cost category:** medium.
Paper	If you have a ready supply of waste paper (newsprint or similar) then it can be worth investing in a shredding machine and using paper as bedding. Paper rots down quickly and easily on the muckheap, so can be very good where space is not available for a large muckheap. However, it can be untidy and tends to blow about the yard when stable doors are opened. **Cost category:** medium-low.
Hemp	Hemp is the "straw" of the hemp plant, which is grown mostly for oil. It looks like finely chopped straw and is similar in use to shavings. Very rarely, some horses eat it and also occasionally some horses can find it dusty in a similar way to straw. **Cost category:** High.
Other products	There are some new kinds of bedding products available, such as chopped, dust-extracted straw and pelleted cardboard. The only way to assess whether these are suitable for your horse is to try them.

pipe insulation, secured in place with strong tape. The door should be low enough for the horse to look over comfortably, but high enough to prevent escape. There should also be somewhere to tie him up safely.

It can be very useful to have a separate covered area that is against a wall for warmth but has two or three sides that are just fenced with post and rails. This makes a well-ventilated living space for a sick horse, away from the main stable block or barn, thus reducing the risk of the spread of infection.

Bedding

The floor in stables is usually of concrete or, occasionally, earth. Concrete is cold, hard, and unyielding and therefore must be covered with something for the comfort and safety of the horse. The traditional bedding is straw, but it is increasingly common to use rubber mats, which provide a more comfortable and warmer surface for the horse to stand (and lie) on. However, there is still a need for some extra bedding, unless the stable is very well drained. The use of a layer of bedding is not only more comfortable for your horse, but facilitates removal of droppings and soaks up any urine. Remember that if he has allergy problems, anything based on straw may be a problem to him. Do not buy large quantities of a new product before you have tried it and are sure that it is suitable for your horse. Refer to the table on the facing page for information on different types of bedding.

Mucking out a straw bed
If you use straw bedding, there will be a large quantity of material to dispose of each day.

Mucking out

In the wild, a horse is constantly on the move and would never stand in its own droppings for any length of time. To keep your stabled horse healthy and the environment pleasant, you should ensure that the stable is mucked out at least once a day if the horse is turned out in the daytime and at least twice a day if he is kept in the stable most of the time. You will also need to skip out (pick up the droppings) as often as possible. There are two basic methods for keeping a stable clean: full muck out and deep litter.

Full muck out

This is the best method for keep down fumes, but it is labour-intensive. Remove all the droppings and all of the wet bedding every day. If possible, leave the floor to dry and air while the horse is not in the stable.

Natural grazing
Grazing grass is the natural way for a horse to spend the majority of his time. The company of other horses turned out together replicates, to some extent, a herd situation.

Deep litter

Remove the droppings frequently, adding a fresh layer of bedding on top daily. Remove all the bedding every few days. You can minimize the smell from a deep litter bed by using a proprietary disinfectant powder, on the floor under the first layer of bedding and between layers. There are some very good products on the market that are designed specifically for equine use. In fact, some are specifically designed for killing organisms, such as influenza or ringworm, that may affect horses. These products come in powder or liquid form; the powder is particularly effective for absorbing odours.

Grazing and fields

For health and happiness, a horse needs to spend at least part of the time outdoors so that it can move freely and gently exercise in the way that nature intended. The most useful regime for most horse owners is one in which the horse is turned out all day and brought into the stable at night. This allows plenty of freedom, but the horse can be bought in early or turned out late to allow for riding and can also be given supplementary feeds when necessary.

It is important to choose the pasture, field, or paddock for your horse's turn-out with care. First, the field must be big enough for the number of horses it contains. The old adage of one horse per acre is a good starting point. But this does not mean entirely that you can keep one horse healthy if you only have one acre of land. As we have seen, horses are herd animals and it is rare

that a horse will be happy living on his own – so he needs a companion. This pushes the land requirement up to two acres. This means that you can divide the land into two parcels and use one and rest one, which is a much better system. A small pony may need slightly less room than a horse and, if necessary, you can divide up the land even more and rotate the ponies around the enclosures. Moreover, if the grass grows well and the ponies are becoming too fat, you have the option of confining them to a small area, and so avoiding the risk of laminitis (see page 132). Indeed, if you have plenty of land and keep ponies, then you would do well to enclose one or two small paddocks. The ponies can then be confined in the spring and summer and a hay crop taken off the main land.

The right conditions

The field should be reasonably flat – although a slight slope will allow for good drainage and a steeper slope will at least provide more intensive exercise for your horse to build up muscle. If you are on clay soil, drainage is even more important. Wet areas should have land drains put in. These are pieces of pipe or channels of gravel that are laid just under the surface and take up excess water until it can drain away naturally. In the field, just as in the stable, horses like to be near other horses, and in a situation where they can watch things going on. One horse I know, spent so much time watching the boats on the canal that ran alongside his field that he had to have his supplementary feeding increased to compensate for the extra exercise he was

Winter feeding
Supplementary feeding is essential to preserve good health and body weight in winter, particularly when snow covers the grass. Placing the hay on the ground allows the horses to feed in a natural way.

getting. Install a water trough in a place where the ground is as dry as possible or surround it with a layer of bark chippings or similar to provide a dry surface on which the horses can stand to drink. The trough should always be kept clean, full and free from ice.

Field and shelter

It is important that even if your horse is stabled at night, the field allows shelter from the prevailing winds and unexpected storms. Your horse must be able to do as he would in the wild and find shelter until conditions improve. A properly designed field shelter is the ideal but a good thick hedge can serve just as well.

Supplementary feeds

In snowy or icy weather or in long periods of bad weather when there just is no grass, a horse turned out will need additional hay to be fed in the field. This can be done in piles on dry spots or in a cattle feeder or in nets. The safest method, although possibly the most wasteful, is on the ground. Hay seeds can fall into the horse's eyes from a cattle feeder and nets always pose a threat of a horse getting a foot caught. If you need to feed a hard feed then you will either have to feed all the horses in the field (from buckets placed well apart) or bring your horse out of the field while he eats.

TROUBLESOME PLANTS

The following list includes plants that are harmful to horses and those that may reduce the quality of the grazing. Remove these plants if you find them on your grazing land.

Beech *(Fagus sylvatica)*	The fruit (beech mast) are poisonous to horses.
Box *(Buxus sempervirens)*	Often used for formal hedges in gardens.
Bracken *(Pteridium)*	Not usually eaten by horses but best pulled up and burned because it spreads and wastes valuable grazing.
Buttercups *(Ranunculus* species*)*	Not usually eaten but the taste can be altered by weedkillers and may then be eaten.
Daffodil *(Narcissus* species*)*	Usually confined to gardens but can be eaten if found growing wild.
Deadly nightshade *(Atropa belladonna)*	Can be eaten accidentally by horses browsing a hedgerow.
Foxglove *(Digitalis purpurea)*	Common in paddocks, but not usually eaten.
Hemlock *(Conium maculatum)*	The young shoots, which appear in spring, are sometimes eaten, the whole plant is deadly.
Holly *(Ilex aquifolium)*	The poisonous berries are sometimes eaten.
Horse chestnut *(Aesculus hippocastanum)*	Horses can eat the leaves, but not the fruit (conkers).
Ivy *(Hedera helix)*	Small amounts seem to be eaten with no harm, but should not be eaten in quantity.
Laburnum *(Laburnum anagyroides)*	Usually found only in gardens, but should be removed if near a grazing area.
Oak *(Quercus* species*)*	The consumption of large quantities of acorns can cause colic and may be fatal. Some animals crave acorns and if this is the case they must be swept up and removed or the animals moved to another field.
Privet *(Ligustrum)*	Popular hedging that is poisonous to horses.
Ragwort *(Senecio jacobaea)*	A pernicious weed, common in Great Britain, that can be fatal if eaten by a horse. It should be pulled up and burned.
Yew *(Taxus baccata)*	Traditionally grown in churchyards, poisoning is so rapid the animals can be found dead with the plant still in its mouth.

Maintaining the grazing

It is important to maintain the grass in good condition. This will mean either picking up the droppings regularly, or on a larger area, using a harrow and spreading them. Resting the field regularly will be useful too. In wet weather horses can wear bald patches in the ground (poaching), and a useful, money saving tip, is to spread the seeds, that fall from hay onto this ground. New grass will grow when the weather improves.

Poisonous plants

It is vital to check any field in which you are considering allowing your horse to graze for poisonous plants. Checks should also be made regularly on fields you are already using, because seeds of poisonous plants can blow in and sprout at any time. Many garden plants are poisonous and crops may have been sprayed with weedkillers and other toxins. If your horse can reach over into a garden or other cultivated area, you may need to erect a secondary fence a few feet inside your original fence to stop him from eating possibly harmful substances. Buy a good photographic guide to poisonous plants if your knowledge, like most people's is somewhat limited, and dig up and burn anything suspicious. Refer to the table on page 47 for further information.

You should also make efforts to encourage good plants. Dandelions, for example, are highly nutritious for horses and can easily be seeded from elsewhere if you do not have any. Brambles should not be removed from the hedge. Horses love the young leaves and some horses will even eat blackberries, which are rich in Vitamin C. A variety of grasses is very desirable, as are a variety of herbs and other plants.

Extra warmth

Nature provides a very good insulating and waterproofing system for horses. With a full coat most horses and especially ponies are capable of withstanding all but the most extreme winter weather conditions outside, when they can keep warm through constant movement. However, for convenience and cleanliness, many horses are now clipped (see Chapter 3). This means that both in the stable and in the field they will need a blanket (rug) in all but the warmest conditions.

The general rule with blankets is that if you need a coat and your horse is stabled at night he will need a blanket. A clipped horse will need at least one thermal blanket to compensate for the loss of his coat, plus others according

Cooler sheet

Use this type of lightweight blanket to prevent your horse cooling down too quickly and getting chilled after a session of strenuous work or after competition.

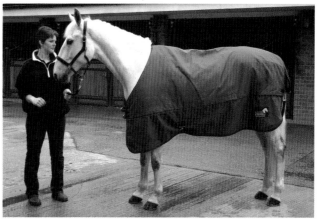

Turn-out blanket

Sometimes known as a New Zealand rug, this waterproof cover keeps your horse dry while turned out. This type of protection makes sure that your horse is dry when brought in at night.

to temperature. If it is raining he needs a waterproof. A horse coming in wet from the field may need a blanket, since a wet horse standing in a stable soon gets cold. If the weather is cold enough for you to need a sweater and a coat, then he needs two blankets (or one very thick one). There are now so many designs and makes of horse blankets on the market that there should be something to suit every

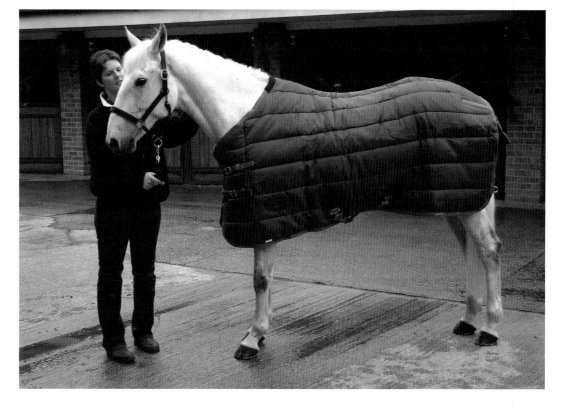

Stable blanket

A quilted blanket provides plenty of warmth for a stabled horse who is unable to generate heat naturally by constant movement.

horse. Most horses are best with cotton next to their skin, especially if they are clipped. This can be topped off with extra warm blankets according to the temperature. A good system is to have several light cotton sheets and to put a clean one every few days. Not only will this cut down on grooming, it will also mean that he always has something clean next to this skin.

Types of halter (headcollar)
An all-purpose traditional leather type (above left) that will break under severe strain is safest for use in horse transporters or for tethering in the stable. A nylon halter (above right) can be used for leading.

Comfort

It is vital that the blanket fits the horse properly and that it does not rub him anywhere. Horse blankets have a tendency to rub the shoulders. This can be prevented by using a specially designed vest underneath the rug. It is important to keep all of your horse's clothing clean. Muddy leg straps can rub the inside of legs, for example, and you might not notice anything until it is bleeding. Waterproof blankets for outdoor use should be kept clean and re-waterproofed at regular intervals.

Halters (headcollars)

Halters should be kept clean, especially if the horse has to wear one in the field. Leather halters, kept well oiled, are always preferable to synthetic ones. Leather will break if the horse gets caught up, for example, in the hedge, avoiding the risk of neck injury if he panics. Leather generally rubs less than nylon. However, if you are only using the halter to take the horse to and from the field, then nylon is perfectly acceptable. For traveling in a van or trailer, you should always use a leather halter and the rope should be attached to a small length of bailer twine or other string and not tied directly to the metal tie ring (see Tip, page 41).

Feeding

Grass and other herbage is the natural food for horses, but fed only on this, they would not be able to cope with the amount of work that we require of them. Although in the distant past the horse would have wandered around finding the best grasses, he now cannot do this, and we have to give him some help to achieve optimum nutrition.

Patterns of feeding

The horse is a "trickle feeder" – feeding almost continuously throughout the day. In the wild horses naturally move considerable distances in the course of a day, finding grass and herbage to eat. Periodically they stop and graze then move on to find more grass elsewhere and graze again. A horse will eat whatever food is available; his instinct tells him to make the most of what is on offer – tomorrow there may be no food at all. To give a greedy pony a big net of hay and a bucket of feed and expect him to make it last all day will not therefore work at all. His feed must be divided up into as many "meals" as is practical and you must try to have some hay available for him to pick at all the time.

Obviously, overweight horses should not be fed as much hay as they would eat, so this too, should be divided into portions that are given at regular intervals during the day. The right amount for your horse can be difficult to

Constant feeding
Wild horses and ponies, such as these ponies in the Camargue region of France, eat small quantities of low-energy food throughout the day to meet their nutritional needs.

judge, but start with the amount recommended by the feed manufacturer and then adjust later according to changes in his general condition, workload, and energy levels.

The compound feed revolution

Horses have always been fed according to whatever was available locally, for example, until the mid 20th century, horses in Great Britain were mainly fed on oats and hay with some bran. Cavalry horses were given oats and barley. Dray horses were often fed brewers' grains, a by-product of the brewing industry. In North America horses have long been fed alfalfa, which is widely available. Nowadays, there are numerous companies around the world making a myriad of different compound foods for every type of horse. The advantage of these feeds is that you know you will be giving your horse the same mixture every day and the quality, designed by a nutritionist, will always be the same. All proprietary feeds have vitamins and minerals added, so you need not worry about your horse being deficient in any particular nutrient. The disadvantage of compound feeds is that they almost always

ALTERNATIVES TO COMPOUND FEEDS

Hay	Hay should ideally be harvested without having been rained upon. If hay is slightly wet during baling, it will generate heat when stacked and will then be "mow burned" and not at all pleasant to smell. Mow burned hay or that which is moldy, dusty, or black should not be used for horses. If you cannot smell summer meadows when you open the bale, then it is not the best hay available.
Haylage	This is semi-dried hay that is packed into airtight plastic bales. This works very well for horses, as it is palatable and of consistent quality. It is, however, much more expensive than hay.
Cereals	You can buy very good quality pure cereals for horses. Oats are a traditional food for horses. They are relatively low in energy and high in fiber. Oats are fed "rolled" or "naked". Rolled oats are crushed for easier digestibility; naked oats are the separated kernels fed without the husk. Naked oats are considerably higher in energy and suitable only for the fit competition horse. Barley can be added or used instead if the horse needs to put on more weight or is finding that oats provide too much energy. Barley is often processed by cooking, steaming, or other processes to make it easier to digest.
Chaff	Chaff, which is chopped straw or hay, sometimes with added alfalfa, can be a useful addition to a cereal-based diet. Try to buy a brand which is not too heavily molassed as this sometimes hides a poor-quality product. Chaff stops greedy feeders bolting their food and bulks out the food of those that are too fat or are confined to the stable because of problems such as laminitis.
Fruit and vegetables	Horses love apples, pears, carrots, and most root vegetables, particularly in wintertime, when they relish something fresh and juicy. Carrots should always be split lengthways and not chopped widthways into round pieces that can choke a horse. Apples and pears should also be treated the same way.

contain substances that the horse would not naturally eat. All kinds of by-products are put together with cereals that may have been be treated to keep down the dust (and therefore might have been of an inferior quality) and various synthetic substances. This is not to say that compound feeds are unsafe for your horse, just that some of them are definitely not very natural.

A natural feeding regime

If you want to try a natural approach, you should first ensure that you have the best quality hay that you can find. It is increasingly easy to buy organic hay – that is, hay from fields that have not been treated with pesticides or artificial fertilizers. The disadvantage is that there may be unwanted weeds in the hay and it should be inspected thoroughly for this reason. Perhaps the best hay is that which has not been treated excessively with chemicals, but has been produced with horses in mind. You may have to spend some time researching reliable local suppliers for such a product.

Vitamins and minerals

If feeding pure cereals, you should add a good vitamin and mineral supplement. This is because cereals are likely to have been grown on chemically treated land, which results in reduced vitamin and mineral content. If you are feeding a compound feed, there is no need to add a supplement. Many horses are fed a number of different and often largely unnecessary supplements. However, a horse whose diet is restricted to grass or just hay and cereals will probably need a calcium supplement. Limestone flour is the best way to supply this. Administer this according to the manufacturer's instructions. If you are unsure about whether your horse is receiving adequate or appropriate nutrition, consult your vet.

Salt

All horses need salt. In the wild they would supply their needs by licking earth or tree bark. Horses with a heavy workload or those in very warm climates need extra salt in their feed and a salt lick in the stable or in the field.

Probiotics

The functioning of the horse's gut is dependent on a population of healthy microorganisms (flora), which ensure proper digestion. Probiotics help to

TIP

While it is less wasteful to feed a horse with hay in a hay net, it is nevertheless more natural to feed him on the ground. It is also more natural to tip his compound feed onto the top of his hay ration, not to give it in a bucket or manger, but again this could prove wasteful.

Mineral lick
Many horses enjoy licking a mineral block in hot weather. It is important to make sure, however, that your horse is not allowed to do this to excess.

maintain the correct balance of gut flora. The balance can be upset by the administration of antibiotics (which kill beneficial bacteria as well as harmful organisms) and stress. Probiotics can be useful for daily feeding to horses who wind-suck and therefore have a predisposition to colic or for competition horses that get stressed about traveling or competing.

Herbal treats

Herbs, especially if they are fresh picked, are often a particular treat for a horse. Do ensure that you know the identification of whatever you are using and that it is picked from a clean, unpolluted place – not the roadside. For details of which herbs might benefit your horse, see Chapter 8.

Water and watering

It is vital that your horse has access to clean water at all times. This may be in a trough in the field or could be from a clean stream that does not have a

Natural grooming
In the wild horses groom themselves by rolling on the ground and by rubbing on trees. Most domestic horses enjoy a good roll, especially when first turned out.

sandy bed (horses can suck up sand when they drink and get a form of colic from this). Buckets are the usual way to provide water in the stable. Automatic waterers save time and effort, but it can be difficult to know how much a horse has drunk (or not drunk) if this method is used.

Feed storage

It is important that horse feed is kept in clean conditions and kept free from contamination from vermin. Bins can be plastic or metal and should have well-fitting lids. Hay should be stored off the ground if possible and kept dry. Once open, a bale of haylage should be used within five days.

Grooming

Grooming is essential to the health of a horse. It removes parasites and helps to distribute natural oils through the coat. Roaming free, horses "groom" each other and will roll, often several times a day, thus grooming themselves. Denied the opportunity to roll, possibly by blankets and sometimes not having enough quality time with other horses, your horse is reliant on you to carry out this vital function. The stabled horse, who may be fed a somewhat artificial diet, will also need to excrete more toxins through his skin, and grooming will assist this process.

If your horse is living out during the winter, remove as little grease from his coat as possible. Grease is his natural protection in wet weather. However, mud should be removed for several reasons. First, left under the saddle or bridle, it will rub and may cause soreness. Secondly, you need to see what is under the mud, such as minor cuts and grazes. Grooming is a great bonding experience for horse and owner and should not therefore be rushed or neglected even when time is short.

Washing

Washing need not be part of your regular grooming routine. However, you may wish to do this occasionally when extra cleanliness is required – for example, for a show, especially if your horse is a gray. Unless the weather is warm, it should be done indoors. The best method is to use warm water and a special shampoo designed for horses. Be sure to rinse his coat thoroughly, finishing off with a rinse containing a cooled nettle or rosemary herbal infusion to add extra shine (see page 153). Hosing down may be the only way to remove wet mud from a horse coming in from the field. However, do not do this if there is any risk of your horse becoming chilled.

GROOMING ROUTINE

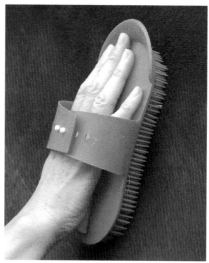

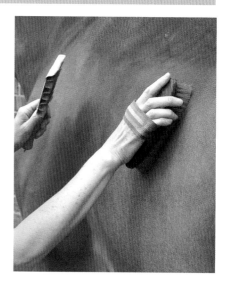

1 Pick out the feet, checking the shoes and the general condition of the foot as you do so. If the feet are caked with mud, this can be washed off with a hose or with a bucket of water and a stiff brush.

2 Loosen mud and dander from the coat with a stiff-bristled dandy brush or rubber or plastic curry comb using circular movements. In dry weather, he may only need brushing over lightly to remove stains. A clean stabled horse may not need this stage.

3 Remove the loosened dirt and hairs with a soft-bristled body brush. Use long stokes to give the coat a good shine. Do not, however, use a body brush on a horse living out in the winter, as it may remove too much oil from the coat.

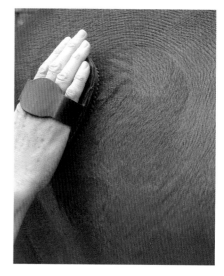

4 As you work, clean the body brush periodically with a metal comb. Use the body brush on the face and legs, which may be too sensitive for the dandy brush. For an extra shine, give his coat a polish with a stable rubber (an old towel will suffice).

5 Use the body brush to groom the mane and tail. When grooming the tail, take a small section at a time in one hand and brush through several times to remove debris and tangles.

6 Horses with short coats and those that are clipped really appreciate a "massage" with a rubber curry comb or rubber brush with long soft "bristles". This encourages circulation to the skin and distributes the natural oils through the coat.

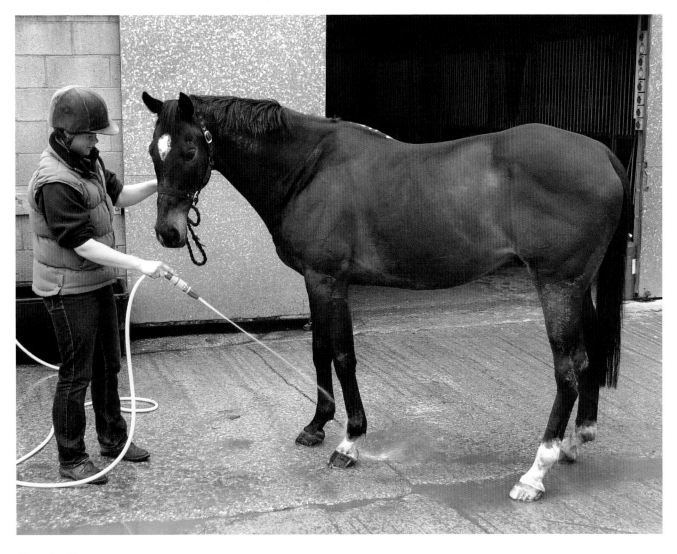

Hoof oil

The healthy horse should not need regular applications hoof oil. His hoof generates all the lubrication it needs and oil could interfere with the natural "breathing" of the hoof. The only exception might be in constantly wet conditions, in which an application of hoof oil could help to provide a waterproof barrier and prevent the hooves cracking when they dry out. However, for special occasions such as showing, an application of hoof oil will help your horse to look smart and will do no harm. See also Hoof infections, page 141.

Hygiene

Always keep your brushes clean, washing them regularly in warm water to which several drops of tea tree oil has been added. Do not share brushes between several horses.

Hosing down
Legs and feet that are caked with mud are most easily cleaned by hosing down. You can then clearly see the condition of the hooves.

3

Exercise and Fitness

In their natural state horses move around for most of the day and possibly some of the night. Confined in a stable for at least part of the day, a horse needs additional exercise if he is to avoid becoming stiff and overweight, and losing muscle tone. Indeed, it can be dangerous for a horse to stand in a stable for several days in a row, unless it is absolutely necessary because of illness or injury.

Even a sick horse can benefit from being led out in hand for as much as the vet allows. Standing motionless or almost motionless for hours on end slows down the circulation, which can lead to a build up of toxins. When a horse stands for any length of time (as in a human being confined to bed) muscle tone is lost, and this in turn weakens the whole body. When the horse starts to work again, he will be more susceptible to injury. He will also be vulnerable to cold when he first goes out if the weather is bad.

Fitness for the job

The level of fitness your horse needs is very much dependent on the job he is required to do. For example, a child's pony does not require the same reserves of speed and stamina as a racehorse. There is also the temperament and type to consider. A hardy pony, used mainly for gentle leisure riding, who keeps himself fairly active in the field does not require a specific program of fitness training for him to be able to complete his work satisfactorily. However, if he is going off for a week's trekking or trail-riding and will be ridden there for several hours every day, he will require more work in the weeks preceding in order to prepare him to cope adequately with the workload. A horse that is to compete in an eventing competition in three months' time, for example, requires a much more rigorous and well-planned program to ensure that he will be able to cope on the day. This should include a mixture of different types of work, including later in his training, galloping and jumping. His feeding regime needs to change to accommodate the additional work, and he may also be clipped, further increasing his food requirements.

So how do you assess your horse's fitness to do any particular job? If you are a top-class competitor, you will already be familiar with the indicators of peak fitness. However, these people make up a very small part of the horse-owning population and the rest of us need more guidance. It is to be hoped that you will have purchased your horse with his eventual job in mind. If you want to go eventing, especially if you are aiming for any degree of success in competition, you will not buy a heavy horse or a pony. You will buy a Thoroughbred or a warmblood, such as a Hanoverian, who will have the potential heart and lung capacity to be trained up to peak fitness for his job. If you only want to go riding once a week, then the degree of fitness achieved by just being in the field on the other days will probably be sufficient exercise to allow him to do this job.

Assessing fitness

Fitness in a horse shows in its ability to carry out fast or strenuous work and to recover from the effort reasonably quickly. Racehorses will usually blow hard after a race (breathing quickly and heavily) but they usually rapidly regain their normal rate of breathing. By contrast, if you give an unfit horse

BEFORE YOU START

Before you embark on a fitness regime with your horse, you should ask yourself the following questions:

■ What do I want him to be able to do, and is he the right type of horse for this job?

■ Is he completely sound and otherwise in good health?

Natural exercise
Horses exercise themselves naturally given enough room and time in the field.

a sudden bout of strenuous work, he will take considerably longer to recover – maybe more than an hour and you will know that he is not yet ready for that level of exercise.

Muscle tone is another good guide to general fitness levels. As you increase your horse's workload to get him fit for a competition or event, or simply for more regular leisure work, you will slowly begin to see more definition in his muscles. His girth (or cinch) may well reduce a hole or two. This does not necessarily mean he is losing weight, because you will presumably be increasing his food to match the increase in his workload. It just means that his flab is disappearing and the muscle is toning up. With increasing fitness, he will recover more quickly from exertion and will probably be more lively when you first get on him. However, this is not always the case and some seasoned competition horses become quiet when they are really fit. It seems as if they know that they are settling down to the job!

Sweating is not a very accurate guide to a horse's fitness. Factors such as the temperature and the amount of coat a horse is carrying affect sweating. Also, some horses by nature sweat more than others. Often horses of a highly strung nature will sweat up simply in anticipation of the forthcoming event or even just the mere fact that they are being tacked up to be ridden can affect them. Some very fit horses sweat under pressure, no matter how fit they are. It is worth noting that sweating while at rest in cool conditions can be a sign that your horse is unwell.

Healthy feet

The essential prerequisite for fitness training is that your horse's feet should be in good order, and for this you will need the advice of a good farrier. A farrier who just comes to fit shoes is not the one you are looking for. You need an expert, who thoroughly understands the workings of the horse's body, and who is capable of ensuring that your horse is as well balanced as his conformation will allow. A horse whose feet are well cared for is much less likely to go lame under the strain of regular work.

The effects of poor shoeing

Problems with a horse's feet or with the way in which he is shod can cause lameness. If the foot is left for a long time to grow, the horse adapts the way in which he uses his body to allow for the extra length of hoof. When the hooves are eventually trimmed, he has to make a sudden adjustment to a completely new way of moving that can cause strain and perhaps more serious injury. If he loses a shoe and you continue to work him without that shoe while waiting for the farrier, you will similarly alter his pattern of going. Incidentally, if you use a farrier whose shoes constantly fall off even though your horse appears to have reasonable feet, then get another farrier. The average horse with good feet keeps his shoes on for the five or six weeks between shoeing.

Working without shoes

Horses need to wear shoes to stop excessive wear of the hoof when worked on paved (or metalled) roads and other hard surfaces. However, in many cases a horse can go without shoes and this is often the best solution. Small ponies work well without shoes and, of course, cause less damage should they tread on children's toes! Any horse working mainly off-road or who is turned out may be better off unshod. Working without shoes should be started gradually if the horse has been shod before. He may be footsore to begin with, but gradually his feet will grow harder. Even when his feet are hard, try

THE STRUCTURE OF THE FOOT

The pedal bone, which carries the weight of the body, is suspended from the inside of the wall of the hoof by the laminae. The wall grows downward constantly from the coronet. If the wall is allowed to grow long or if the hoof is badly shod, the horse's weight will not be correctly distributed over the hoof and the consequent imbalance may place strain on the joints and tendons of the leg.

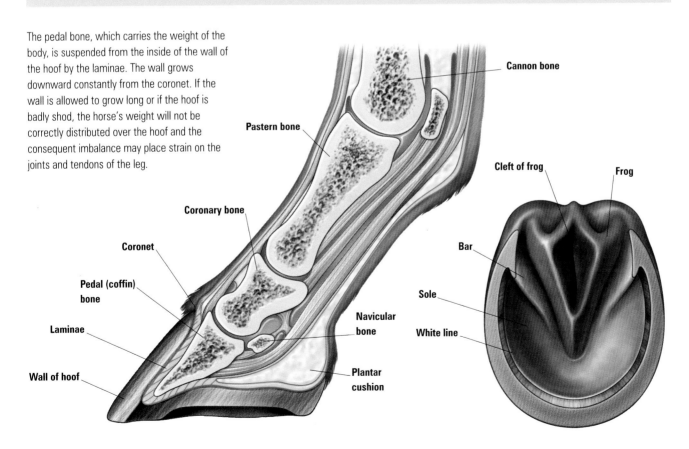

Cannon bone

Pastern bone

Cleft of frog

Frog

Coronary bone

Coronet

Bar

Pedal (coffin) bone

Sole

Navicular bone

Laminae

White line

Wall of hoof

Plantar cushion

to avoid very stony tracks, and be careful of wearing away too much foot on paved roads. A note of warning should be sounded here. If you want to keep your horse without shoes, you must nevertheless have the farrier check his feet every six to eight weeks. Your unshod horse will need to have his feet trimmed properly to suit his conformation and type. There are a number of methods of foot trimming that have been given wide publicity that are supposed to be "natural" and can supposedly be done by the owner who has been on a short course. Many experienced farriers and vets have criticized these methods and they are not to be recommended.

Soundness for jumping

The horse's body takes a great deal of strain when he is ridden. If he engages in activities that include jumping – whether in competion or as an element of leisure riding, he will experience more strain – strain not only on his joints and muscles but also on the tendons and ligaments that bind the two together. Although horses would normally jump streams and small obstacles in the wild, they would not of course be carrying a weight on their back. Lifting their bodyweight, plus that of a rider over a fence several feet high

Taking the strain
Jumping fences of competition height carrying the weight of a rider demands a high level of strength and fitness from a horse.

requires very strong leverage in the limbs, especially the hind limbs. His front legs must take the whole weight albeit for a few seconds when landing over a fence. You cannot start to train a horse that is even slightly lame: the extra strain is likely to exacerbate any problem rapidly. Take the time to observe carefully the way your horse stands and moves before you consider increasing his workload. See Chapter 1 for advice on recognizing the signs of lameness. If you are not sure if your horse is lame, seek professional advice.

Clipping

Clipping takes off some of the horse's coat so that he can work for longer without getting sweated up and stressed by heat that cannot be lost through a thick coat. While clipping is unnatural, because it inevitably means that blankets will have to be used to replace the missing coat, it is nevertheless better for a horse with a thick winter coat to be clipped if he is undertaking strenuous work or is involved in competition. There are a number of different methods of clipping, from taking off just a sweat patch up the front of the chest and under the neck (this works well on children's ponies) to a full clip, which is for competition horses.

Do not underestimate the amount of heat a horse loses from the parts of his body that are clipped. As well as needing blankets, he may need extra food to replace the calories that he is using keeping warm.

Tack

The other important item to consider is that your tack all fits well. A horse that has not done serious work recently will soon be rubbed by ill-fitting tack. See Chapter 4 for detailed advice on ensuring that your tack is suitable and fits properly.

Starting work

As for humans, walking is superb exercise for horses. If you can ride up and down some hills, so much the better. It is a very individual decision as to when to start trotting a previously unfit horse and, similarly, when to start cantering and you should be guided by your observations of your horse's responses. If he blows (that is to say breathes rapidly and in a laboured way) for more than a few minutes after you have been trotting, then it is not time to start cantering. Very fit racehorses often blow for some time after completing a race, but this is because of the extreme nature of the effort required on such occasions. Generally, you should not get your horse blowing on a regular basis for more than a few minutes at a time and if he is constantly breaking out in a sweat after he is back in his stable, then you need to reduce the intensity of work until he has become fitter through a more gradual program.

A varied program

A fitness program for your horse shouldn't be seen as a chore that involves tedious, repetitive work. There are lots of enjoyable and varied riding activities that you can use to get your horse to a high level of fitness without either of you getting bored in the process.

CHIROPRACTIC TREATMENT

There are many people who believe that before you start getting a horse fit, it is advisable to arrange for him to have one or more sessions of chiropractic treatment (see page 186). An unfit horse may have flabby muscles that do not support his skeleton in proper alignment and this should be corrected before he starts serious work. If he strains a muscle in training any consequent muscle spasm will make it much harder for the chiropractor to correct the horse's alignment. A chiropratic treatment at this stage may also identify hidden strains or other problems that have gone unnoticed and that would benefit from treatment before the horse starts work.

General work: To improve your horse's fitness while leisure riding, try to include some uphill work, vary your routes, and include different surfaces, if you can. Do not always go into trot in the same place and, if possible, ride with different company. Not only does this keep your horse alert and interested, but he learns how to behave around unfamiliar horses, which is very important.

While riding along quiet roads, paths, or trails, you can take the opportunity to practice exercises for increasing suppleness. For example, providing there is no likelihood of traffic, you can half pass across the path or trail, first at the walk and then at the trot, ensuring that you use the edge to establish the correct bend and that you perform the movement correctly. To add further variety to your rides, you can work on upward and downward transitions and on your halting. In addition, you can also practice shouldering-in, using a fence or hedge along the trail, instead of the side of the arena (or menage), to establish the movement.

Riding for leisure and fitness
Make your leisure rides in open country an opportunity to develop your horse's fitness and your own technique by practicing schooling exercises on your route.

Keep it interesting
It is important to plan your schooling work so that your horse does not get bored. Make a point of varying the sequence of exercises and introduce new challenges regularly.

The importance of lunging

Lunging (longeing) is good exercise for a horse. It provides an opportunity for you to observe his way of going if there is no one available to ride him for you. It is also a useful way of maintaining fitness in a pony when the owner has become too heavy to ride him. Be sure to use the right tack and leg protection.

Pool work

If you are lucky enough to have access to an equine pool, you can give your horse the opportunity to swim, which provides a different type of exercise from riding.

Arena (school) work: Schooling need not be boring. It is certainly an excellent way to improve your horse's fitness and your own riding technique. Teach your horse some of the dressage movements mentioned above and use them to vary your work.

Jumping practice: Gridwork – working over poles on the ground or at a low height and set at different distances apart – is the foundation for jumping. Even horses who are intended for a career in dressage can benefit from it. It makes the horse pick up his feet and extend his paces as he reaches for the next pole. If you intend your horse to have a job where he needs to jump, then do not just jump him endlessly over fences in the arena. He should learn to jump many different obstacles, including natural jumps, such as logs, low hedges, and streams, that you may encounter when riding along trails or in open country. However, take care never to overface him – that is, to present him with a jump that is beyond his present experience. If he makes mistakes or loses his confidence or indeed gets bored in the early years, he may never learn to enjoy his jumping again. If you let him get bored, you may find that he stops jumping or starts knocking fences down.

A place for horse (hot) walkers

The use of a horse walker, in which the horse circles at walking pace in a rotating frame, is not an ideal exercise method. However, it can be useful in a large establishment where it is not possible to ride every horse daily.

A peak of fitness
Endurance riding, particularly at competition level, demands a high degree of fitness of both horse and rider. Such fitness levels can only be achieved by months of careful preparation.

Swimming: Horses usually love swimming. If you have an equine pool near to you then do try it. This form of exercise builds muscle and improves fitness without strain on the joints. It makes a welcome change for the horse – and it keeps his coat clean! Swimming is particularly beneficial for horses that cannot be ridden for some reason.

Competition preparation: If you intend to use your horse in competition, whether in small, local events or larger shows, be sure to vary his work and don't just focus on his specialty. For example, if you are training your horse for show jumping, enter him in some novice dressage competitions and take him in a show class or two. He may not win, but the change will ensure that he does not get stale. He will go to his next "proper" competition in a good frame of mind, because he will not know what is in store for him when he sets off in the van or trailer. Similarly, some relaxed leisure riding will help to keep him interested. His mental fitness is almost as important as his physical fitness and will ensure that he enjoys his work, which in turn will give you more pleasure.

Time for work

Fitness is only achieved by regular work. This should be about an hour a day, but should be done on six days a week. When he is fit enough, you could also undertake an occasional longer ride for variety and to build up his stamina. On the seventh day, turn out your horse for a few hours or just walk him out in hand for about 20 minutes. It is important to keep to this type of regular routine, if you want to get results.

Time for rest

It is vital that you plan your exercise session to allow your horse time to cool down and relax, particularly after strenuous schooling work, before you put him away in the stable. At the end of the session walk him until he has stopped blowing and his breathing is relaxed. He may be sweaty, especially on a hot day, so be sure to put on a cooler sheet (see page 49) and keep him out of drafts until he has dried off in order to prevent muscle stiffness the next day. Do not let him drink cold water immediately; this could bring on an attack of colic.

STRETCHING ROUTINE

1 The easiest stretch to teach your horse, is when you give him a carrot or other treat, hold it between his front legs. You may have to show him the carrot first and guide his head down. This stretches the top of his neck from the withers to the poll. Some horses will even stand like this when they see you with a treat, when they are familiar with this exercise.

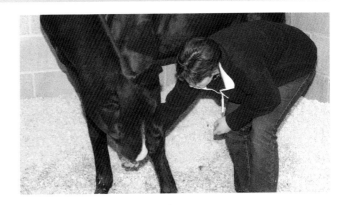

2 Next, stretch the sides of his neck. Stand him near a wall and hold the treat in the girth area so that he stretches around to reach it. If you do not have him against a wall he will just turn his whole body around. Turn him around and do the same on the other side.

3 Stretch the front leg by grasping the lower leg below the knee and at the fetlock joint and stretching it forward. To stretch the foreleg back hold round the cannon bone and lift as for picking out the hooves. Move the leg gently back and forward. Repeat on both sides.

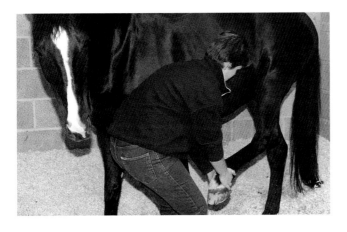

4 For a hind limb stretch, grasp the leg around the pastern and pull the leg forward and up. Stretch both sides equally.

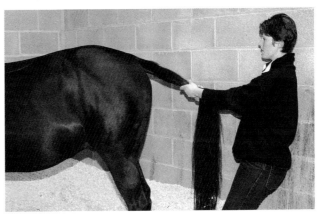

5 Stretch the back by grasping the tail around the dock and gently leaning back while rocking the tail from side to side.

Stretching

Stretching is a valuable aid to conditioning your horse. After all human athletes do a stretching routine, so why shouldn't equine athletes! However, unlike humans, who often stretch as part of a warm-up routine, your horse should do his exercises after work or after massage or when he comes in from the field (although not if he has been standing around on a cold day). Stretching encourages flexibility and athletic ability, but you must take care to do this properly. It is important to remember that any stretch should be done gently. If the horse shows any sign of discomfort you should stop immediately. Limbs should always be stretched in the natural way that they can move. Movement should always be slow and gentle but firm. You must grasp the limb firmly and with confidence so that the horse trusts you.

Relaxing after work
At the end of a strenuous schooling session, let your horse relax and cool down. Loosen the reins and allow him to walk at his own pace until his breathing has returned to normal.

Massage after work

As your horse gets fit and, indeed, when he is fit and in full work, he will benefit greatly from a massage after work. Massage encourages the circulation to the muscles and enhances the toning effects of exercise. You do not have to be an expert horse masseur to be able to give your horse a great deal of benefit. In addition, by carrying out regular massage you will develop a better "feel" for your horse's body, making you better able to spot a hard or hot muscle that may have been damaged during work.

MASSAGE ROUTINE

1 Start your massage with the neck. Rocking thre crest gently back and forward is very soothing for your horse. It replicates to some degree the feeling of the mare putting her head over the foals neck, which is very comforting.

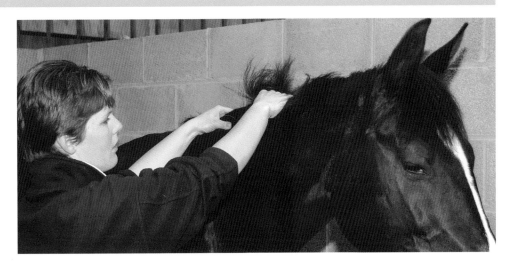

2 Work very carefully over bony areas such as the shoulder in order to avoid causing discomfort. Use a stroking action in these areas rather than kneading.

3 Areas that are well covered with muscle (and fat) can be massaged more deeply. The movement should always be outward and downward toward the tail and toward the thigh and hock.

4

The Natural
Rider

Carrying a rider is not a natural activity for a horse. We have become so used to the idea that horses are ridden that it is all too easy to lose sight of the fact that when we get on a horse, we are imposing on him a load that he was not intended to carry. We need to be aware that a horse will go better and be a more comfortable ride if we consider and make allowances for his physical capabilities.

Carrying the load

If you picture the shape and conformation of the horse, you will see that the rider's weight is carried in the middle of his spine. Not only does the horse have to support the rider, but also the weight of the saddle. No wonder that people who manipulate and treat horse's backs often have waiting lists of customers! The health of your horse's back has to be a priority and how you ride has a big impact on this.

THE HORSE'S SPINE

The spine of the horse runs from the top of the head (poll) to the end of the tail and although you might think that it flexes at each of the vertebrae, it is actually rather rigid in most places. The poll is flexible and there is quite a lot of movement in the neck (cervical) vertebrae. The tail, too, especially where it joins the body, is flexible to allow for balance and to enable it to swish to keep off flies. In between there is very little movement, probably less than half an inch (1 cm) in most places. There is just one joint in the spine that allows greater movement – the one just in front of the pelvis, which allows for urination and facilitates foaling.

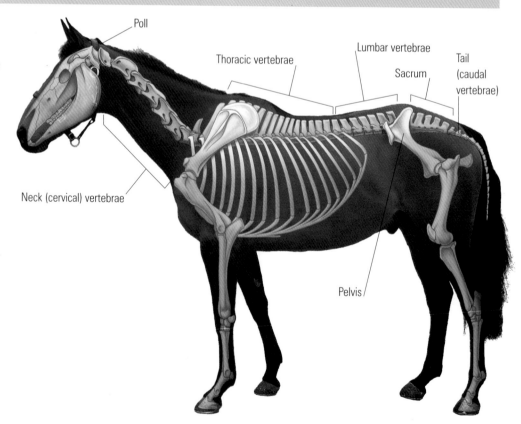

Tack considerations

There are various styles of riding each of which uses different types of saddlery. The two main styles being addressed here are English riding and Western riding.

English saddles

The most usual English saddle is a general purpose one. This is a saddle with a reasonably deep seat and knee rolls on the flaps. The cantle and pommel are higher than the middle of the seat, but not excessively high.

Saddles should always be fitted by an expert – and you need to choose your expert carefully. Even some with qualifications are not sufficiently aware of horse anatomy to make sure a saddle is a completely comfortable fit. Others, who may be more interested in making a sale, may try to persuade you that you can get away with a "near enough" fit. It is also the case that the kind of saddle that suits one horse will not necessarily be the right choice for you and your horse, even if it is endorsed by a well-known rider. The only way to assess the fit of a saddle is by observation.

SADDLE POSITION

It is easy for an inexperienced rider to place the saddle too far back or too far forward. A correctly fitted saddle should naturally settle itself into the right position. A saddle that is hard to place correctly may be a bad fit for your horse. The photographs (right) show a saddle placed too far back so that it presses on the loins (top left); a saddle placed too far forward so that it will interfere with the movement of the shoulder (top right); and a saddle correctly placed for ease of movement and comfort of the horse (bottom left).

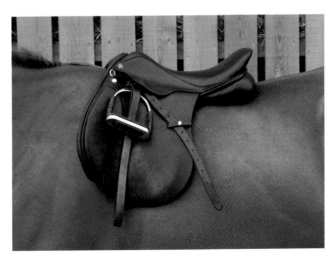
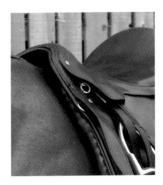

The pommel of the saddle should be well clear of the withers (above).

Fitting considerations

Many saddles are not wide enough for the horse. Horses today are often quite broad in the back, as a result of better nutrition and less work than in the past. However, a saddle that is too wide can be uncomfortable for the horse, too. If the saddle tree is too narrow, there will not be enough space between the bearing surfaces of the saddle. In an extreme case they may even impinge on the spine. Even if the pommel is well clear of the withers, the muscles on each side of the spine, under the front of the saddle can atrophy as a consequence of the constant pressure. This results in loss of sensation in those muscles affected and may lead to other problems, such as further injury being occasioned when nerve sensations are not as good as they should be. Indeed, at post mortem, many horses are shown to have fibrous tissue on the back from constant saddle problems. The gullet of a saddle for even the narrowest horse needs to be a minimum of 2 ½ inches (60 mm) wide, widening farther towards the pommel.

The saddle sits on the horse's back just behind the withers. Adequate clearance of the shoulder usually puts it in a place that is approximately correct. If the saddle is put on the horse's back too far forward it will restrict movement of the shoulder. If the saddle is put too far back, the rider will not be in the right place for the horse's center of balance.

Different disciplines tend to put the saddle in a slightly different place on the horse's back. For example, a rider who is showing a horse in a ridden class and wants to ensure that movement is not hampered by the saddle, will perhaps choose to position the saddle farther back than a rider who is about to undertake a cross-country event and wants to ensure maximum balance. Therefore, it is clear that no one exact place is correct. The correct place to position your saddle is where it is comfortable for the horse and rider.

It is also vital that the bearing surfaces of the saddle fit and are in contact over as wide an area of the horse as possible during use. Put a clean saddle on your horse when he is dirty (but not muddy) with no saddle cloth or pad. When you remove the saddle, the dirt adhering to the underside of the saddle will indicate how much of his saddle is in contact with the back. Incidentally, if your English saddle needs padding underneath it, it does not fit your horse properly. A well-fitting saddle does not need a saddle pad. The only exception to this is the use of a sheepskin underneath the saddle when a horse has particularly sensitive skin.

A traditional and effective way of checking the fit of a saddle is to make sure you can see clearance along the gullet for its whole length. There should also be enough room for three fingers to fit under the pommel. However, just because a saddle meets these requirements, do not assume that it is a good fit. If the tree is too narrow it will restrict free forward movement and may cause discomfort to the horse. Expert saddle fitting in quiet and still surroundings is time and money very well spent.

The girth

When thinking about the saddle, you should also consider the girth. Leather girths should be kept soft and supple and all girths should be very clean. As long as the material of the girth is clean and well kept there is really no advantage of any one type of material over another. A horse with sensitive skin may also react badly to some harsh laundry products and even to the dye in some girths. The girth should fit properly so that in use it is buckled about halfway up the straps, thus allowing plenty of adjustment in both directions.

ADJUSTING THE GIRTH

1 When tightened, a girth of the correct length for your horse buckles about half way up the straps on each side of the saddle. Be sure to pull down the buckle guards after adjusting the girth so that the saddle flap is protected against wear.

2 Feel the tightness of the girth by inserting your fingers underneath. The fit should be snug, without being excessively tight. Always check the girth again after you have been in the saddle for a few minutes. A loose girth can allow the saddle to slip while riding.

SADDLING UP WESTERN STYLE

1 Place your folded saddle blanket in position. Make sure there are no wrinkles that could cause chafing under the saddle and that it covers the withers.

2 Place the saddle on the folded blanket. A Western saddle can be heavy to lift. Make sure that you lower it gently onto the horse's back to avoid alarming him.

3 Adjust the position of the saddle so that it sits comfortably clear of the withers but not too far back on the loins (see page 77). Pull the blanket up into the gullet of the saddle.

4 Bring the cinch under the horse's belly and pass the latigo through the cinch buckle and back through the D ring on the saddle. Tighten to secure the saddle.

5 Wind the latigo back through D ring and pull firmly to secure.

6 Insert the excess length of latigo into the latigo carrier at the front of the saddle.

  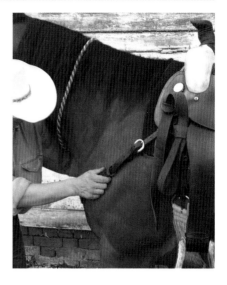

7 Secure the rear cinch to the rear cinch strap. This cinch is occasionally omitted but is necessary to keep the saddle from lifting during roping work.

8 Recheck the tightness of both cinches before mounting.

9 Finally fasten the breastplate, which prevents the saddle from slipping back.

10 Evolved to meet the needs of cowhands for stabilty in the saddle, properly fitted Western tack provides maximum comfort for both horse and rider during long trail rides.

It will also prevent the buckles being off the bottom of the saddle flap, as happens sometimes in small, fat ponies. If this occurs the flesh may be pinched painfully between the buckle and the flap.

Western saddles

Western saddles are designed to carry the rider for many miles at a fairly even pace over all types of terrain. They are supremely comfortable for the rider and should also be supremely comfortable for the horse. While many Western riders like a smart appearance to the saddle with tooling and silver decoration, no amount of decoration will make your horse more comfortable. There are two basic types of saddle – the plain leather working saddle and the show saddle, which is fancier and has a deeper seat and a sloping horn. You might also see a cutting saddle, which has a flatter profile and allows greater freedom of movement for the rider when being used for cattle work.

The fit of a Western saddle has much in common with an English saddle. There should be sufficient clearance over the spine, to allow free movement of the muscles at each side. The saddle should be tried without a saddle pad as described above to check this. Again there should be no interference with the movement of the shoulder and the saddle should not be so long as to press on the loin. On a Western saddle you have to set the angle of the fenders before use. These are the large pieces of leather that cover the stirrup leathers. Badly set fenders will be uncomfortable for you and thus uncomfortable for the horse.

When saddling up Western style it is customary to put a saddle blanket on first. The blanket is usually folded to be around an inch thick. A pad of this thickness may be employed instead. There are two types of girth that may be used. An ordinary Western girth buckles onto the saddle in much the same way as an English girth. The older type is the cinch which has a buckle at both ends, with excess length (known as latigo) being folded into a carrier on the saddle. Sometimes two cinches are used, but a second cinch is only necessary for roping work.

Bits and bridling

Your bridle should fit comfortably somewhere on the middle adjustment holes and care should be taken not to have a browband that is too small and pinches the forehead.

Your bit, whatever it is, should fit neatly in the mouth. It should not be too big or too small – one that is too small will pinch the corners of the mouth and a bit that is too big will rub. An over-heavy bit will bother a young horse and a bit with a joint in the center may pinch a horse with a big tongue. There is a size and shape of bit to fit every horse, but it is best to start with a simple snaffle and work from there. Choose a thick eggbutt snaffle or a snaffle with cheek pieces. Many horses spend their lives happily wearing a snaffle and never need a more severe bit.

Special bridling gadgets

Much money is wasted every year on bits that promise miracles in terms of improving your horse's performance, and do not deliver the promised results. The reason for this is, of course, because no bit, however sophisticated, can make up for lack of basic schooling or an even more fundamental lack of ability, conformation, or experience for the job. In fact, introducing a new bit when the problem lies elsewhere could create even more difficulties.

FITTING AN ENGLISH BRIDLE

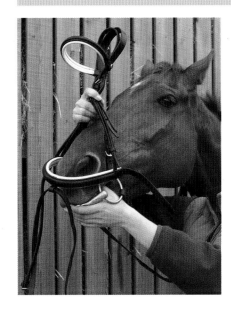 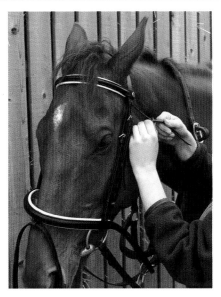 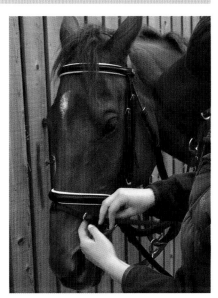

1 Stand to the side of the horse and place the reins over his neck. Holding the cheek pieces above the nose, ask your horse to open his mouth by inserting your thumb into the side of his mouth. As soon as he does so, slip the bit into place.

2 Bring the headpiece gently over his ears. fasten the throat lash (throatlatch) and then the noseband. Be sure to check that the mane and forelock are not uncomfortably caught in the headpiece or browband.

3 Finally check the fit of all parts of the bridle (see Bridle-fitting watchpoints, page 84) and adjust as necessary.

BRIDLE-FITTING WATCHPOINTS

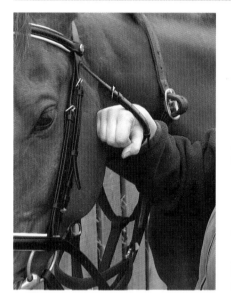

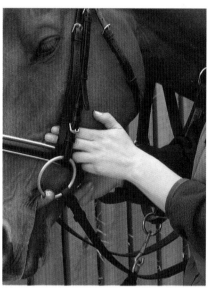

1 It is important for your horse's comfort to make sure that his bridle is correctly fitted. There should be sufficient room to insert your hand sideways between the throat lash and throat.

2 Adjust the cheek pieces so that you can insert your hand underneath. However, these should not be so loose that the bit hangs too low in the mouth. You should be able to fit two fingers under the noseband.

3 Check that you can easily fit your thumb under the browband.

Other bridling "gadgets" also fall into this category of failed miracles. Every new gadget produces a crop of devotees and sells well until it falls from favour and something else comes along. Those tangled heaps of nylon that you see at tack sales were once the latest bridling gimmick costing a great deal of money and now useless without the CD ROM instruction manual and quite frankly probably useless even then.

A few specialized tack items are useful for correcting some problems in horses in the short term. For example, a horse in a dealer's yard may not have the time to go back to basic schooling and learn to move in a better shape. The right gadget may show this horse an improved way of going instantly. However, as the owner of an individual horse, you owe it to him to be patient and gradually work on his outline. In this way, when he works in a new and better shape it will be maintained longer because he will have built up the relevant muscles. Old-fashioned draw reins will sometimes show a young horse that he can actually carry his head lower without falling over. To ride out in a draw rein day after day is not recommended.

FITTING THE WESTERN BRIDLE

1 A Western bridle is fitted in much the same way as an English bridle, holding the head- and cheekpieces over the nose as you insert the bit. In this example, a Western bridle with a single earpiece and a fixed curb bit is shown.

2 Having inserted the bit, pull the head-piece over the ears and the earpiece over one ear. Check the fit as for an English bridle (see facing page).

BOSAL BRIDLE

The bosal is a thick and relatively rigid noseband made from plaited leather, secured by cheek pieces and and earpiece or browband. The mecate (reins), traditionally made from horsehair is fixed to the underside of the bosal. Control is exerted by pressure on the nose and leverage action on the poll. Correctly fitted, the bosal should lie about 4 inches (10 cm) above the nostrils. The underside should be clear of the jaw.

Western bridles

Western riders often use a bitless bridle. In the traditional type, control is achieved by a length of plaited rawhide that goes around the nose and exerts pressure on the nose when the reins are pulled (see Bosal bridle, right). The hackamore is an alternative bitless bridle with metal sidepieces. It is more severe and achieves control through lever action on the nose and poll. Other Western bridles use various types of snaffle or a fixed curb. As with any other bit, there is no need to experiment once a comfortable bit is found and no need to use a more severe bit until you are certain that the problem does not lie elsewhere.

Care of your tack

Tack should be cleaned each time it is used. All leatherwork should be kept soft and supple by diligent care. It should be wiped clean with a damp cloth and then treated with saddle soap or a leather dressing. Bits should be thoroughly washed without detergent and never polished if they are to be put back into the horse's mouth. Check all tack for damage and fit when

Centered seat
For your own and your horse's well-being, it is important to sit centrally and evenly balanced over your horse's spine. Have someone else stand behind you to check your alignment if you are unsure whether you are sitting correctly.

reassembling and each time you tack up your horse. Your saddlery is what is keeping you on the horse (with a modicum of balance and good luck thrown in), so whether you are showing or simply riding for pleasure, it makes good sense to keep it in top condition.

Balanced riding

The horse uses both his muscles and his spine to support the weight of the rider, and through careful riding technique the rider can do much to keep these parts of the horse in good condition. When the rider is sitting on the horse, her weight is supported by the muscles on each side of the spine. It is therefore important that the rider sits with her weight centered evenly over the saddle and thus the horse's spine. Consistently leaning to one side will result in uneven muscle development in the horse and risks possible back pain or lameness. The rider too will suffer back pain if she continually sits to one side.

Uneven weight distribution affects the horse less when he is moving, because the action of forward movement makes it easier for him to adjust to the rider's weight. This does not mean that it matters less that you sit and

MOUNTING WITHOUT STRAIN

When you mount your horse, do you put your foot in the stirrup and then heave your weight up and across his back? You might like to think about the strain that this places on his near side each time and, unless you are very athletic, use a mounting block instead. If you do not have a mounting block, improvise by standing on a bale of straw, for example. Horses soon get used to being mounted in this way and will usually learn to stand still for you.

A friendly start
It is always good practice to "greet" your horse before you mount. This gives him the chance to become accustomed to your voice and physical presence.

ride squarely and in a balanced manner. You should always be conscious of your position and of the ease with which your horse is carrying you. Try to find the opportunity to ride in an arena with mirrors so that you can observe and correct your riding position. When you have established a well-balanced, natural position, it will probably become second nature to you, but it may be a good idea to recheck yourself once in a while.

Too heavy for your horse?

It is important you should not ride a horse for which you are too heavy. A horse's back is very strong, but nevertheless much damage can be done by riding if you are too heavy. As a general guideline, a pony of 13.2 hands can normally carry about 112 pounds (8 stone/50 kg). However, much depends on the build and type of horse; some Thoroughbreds struggle to carry an average-sized adult, while the much smaller Welsh Pony can easily do so in most cases.

Riding philosophies

It is not possible to examine all the many different riding techniques that are "in vogue" today. These include such methods as Thinking Riding, Centered Riding, Natural Riding, and so on. What these have in common is an emphasis on achieving better communication between the horse and rider, so that the horse is treated with greater respect for both his physical and emotional health. This in turn makes riding much better experience for the rider. It is a good idea to go and learn one of these techniques. You will be amazed by the difference it makes to your relationship with your horse and contributes to his overall wellbeing. Here I will try to explain some general ideas that are put forward by all of these methods, and then describe exercises that may help make your riding technique more sensitive to the needs of your horse.

The response to fear

Riding on the back of a horse is an unnatural thing to do – for both the horse and the rider and can lead to fear and tension in both parties. Those who are truly terrified of horses do not usually attempt to ride. However, many normally confident riders can become tense when faced with a difficult or unusual situation, for example, in traffic or when the horse is alarmed by something unusual. Such tension, and in some cases fear, is easily communicated to the horse, who may interpret the sensation of having a tense rider as similar to that of having a predator on his back.

RELAXATION WATCHPOINTS

Ensure you are totally relaxed by following this simple
horseback relaxation routine.

1 Start with your scalp and face,
relax them and your mouth
and see how that feels better.

2 Think about your arms and imagine your
thoughts going down inside them, and then
into your hands. Unclench your fingers if
necessary. Hold the reins lightly but firmly.

5 Relax your tummy and ensure that
your breathing is regular and slow.
Now you are ready to move off.

4 Feel your seat bones
pressing into the saddle
and the contact of your
thigh with the saddle too.

3 Feel down inside your legs,
feel them in your boots and
your boot on the stirrup.

So here is your horse with a frightened and perhaps threatening "thing" hanging on his back, possibly hunched up in an animal-like position. In some cases the rider adds to the horse's alarm by issuing shouts of fear. The horse's natural reaction at this stage is to run – to run as far away from this "predator" as possible, possibly even trying to buck her off at the same time. So the cycle of fear establishes itself. Next time this rider gets on, she is likely to be nervous at first, even on a different horse. A horse that has had a bad experience with a rider will himself be tense and nervous and the circle perpetuates itself.

Relaxed riding

What about changing what happens even before you mount? Start when you first approach your horse. Make sure that your clothing is comfortable and

LOOSEN UP BEFORE YOU START

1 Tension in the arms and shoulders can lead to "hard" hands when you ride. Practice these exercises before you start your ride. Stretch your arm upward and allow it to relax. Repeat for each arm three times.

2 Circle each shoulder forward and then back three times to ease stiffness in the shoulders and neck.

3 Lift both shoulders up toward your ears and then let them drop heavily back down. Repeat three times. This helps to release tension in the upper back and neck. You can stop and repeat these exercises during your ride if you feel tension accumulating again.

that you will not be too hot or too cold. If you are uncomfortable in any way, you will begin to sit stiffly and this subtle change will transfer to the horse and so on. Your horse must be comfortable too. Tack him up carefully, checking that all is properly adjusted.

Do you walk him out of the stable and just get on? What about talking to him first and establishing close contact before you get on his back. Your first contacts before riding set the mood for the riding session. When you are mounted, (see page 86 for advice on mounting without strain) just sit quietly in the saddle for a few minutes. Stroke his neck and just think about tuning in to him. Is he impatient to be off and therefore fidgeting? See if you can send him some calming thoughts. Reassure him that it is safe for you to be on his back and that there is no rush to do anything; meanwhile stroke his neck and keep yourself relaxed.

Tuning in to your horse

Now we can think about this partnership between horse and rider. Is the horse taking you along or are you actually riding him? When you were a beginner, you most likely experienced an overwhelming sense of being taken by the horse. Many people learn in riding schools, in which the horses knows far more about the job than the learner riders. If you are riding a horse like this, do not despair of reversing the roles, they will gradually change as you become more confident.

For the moment, just feel the movement of the horse as he walks beneath you. One and two and three and four – you might like to sing a little song to this rhythm. This will actually help to relax you as you concentrate on fitting the words round the tune. Hold your reins lightly but firmly and think about feeling your horse's mouth on the other end of the rein. Feel the weight of

RETAINING YOUR BEGINNER'S MIND

In her wonderful book *Ride With Your Mind*, Many Wanless talks about the "beginner's mind." She celebrates the joy of learning throughout life. This state of mind is one valued in Zen philosophies and is aptly characterized in the child who is just getting to know ponies and for whom even emptying the muck barrow is a complete delight. If you can find that state of mind and use it in everything that you do with horses, it will immeasurably enhance your enjoyment of riding and general horse care.

his head and feel how he moves it in time to his walk. If for any reason his head is nodding heavily or snatching with the motion, there is probably something wrong and you should seek expert advice. Try to become more aware of your reins so that you can feel part of the whole movement. Your hands should not be bobbing up and down but just gently responding to the movement.

As you progress with your riding, you should always try to maintain this lightness of touch; this relaxed but confident air and a clear mind with no fears. Keep balanced and develop a seat that allows you to "ride" the horse instead of the horse taking you. Always take the time to tune in to your friend – notice whether he is tired or feeling below par or just not able to do what you ask. Respect him and build a loving and confident relationship with him. People say that horses can feel the fear down the reins and this may or may not be the case, but if they can do this, then they can also feel love and reassurance down the reins and this will inspire them to have greater confidence themselves.

Balance and rhythm

Two words that are very important if you want to improve your riding and improve the experience for your horse are "balance" and "rhythm." When you are on your horse's back, you both have to be balanced together in harmony. This is particularly important during those fleeting instances when you are both suspended in the air. If you are unbalanced in any way at these times, it will create stress for both you and your horse. Balance is most crucial during a change of pace (transition). This is when it is easiest to get left behind the forward motion or shot forward in front of a slowing motion. In either case you will lose your balance in the saddle. This makes it more difficult for the horse to move in a natural rhythm underneath your weight on his back.

The following exercise works with the natural rhythm of your horse to help you to keep your balance. Change your breathing so that it is in rhythm with the horse's pace. Practice this in trot by lengthening the trot along one side of the arena and then shortening it along the next. This can also be done along a measured distance along a track, road, or trail. Balance and rhythm are all about the feeling that you get from the horse as he moves beneath you. When you feel in harmony with this movement, then balance and rhythm are well on their way to being established.

STAYING WITH THE MOVEMENT

Behind the movement (above left)

The rider is no longer synchronized with the movement of the horse. When the rider gets "behind the movement" in this way the horse is unbalanced and uncomfortable.

In front of the movement (above)

If you are not constantly "listening" to your horse via your contact through the saddle and reins, you risk being surprised by a sudden change of pace. The horse above has slowed, leaving the rider "in front of the movement" and very insecure in the saddle.

In harmony (left)

Sitting deep in the saddle, moving in harmony with the rhythm of the horse, the rider achieves balance and security in the saddle, which is more comfortable for the horse.

5

Behaviour
Problems

To enable us to live in harmony with our horses, we need to understand the main sources of the problems that commonly occur between horses and humans. The most obvious cause of misunderstanding is that we speak a different language – this is true, but the problem goes much deeper than that. The horse sees his world from an entirely different perspective from humans and uses instinctive responses that do not follow human "logic" to deal with everyday events and unexpected occurrences.

For the horse, nothing much appears to have changed in his communication systems since domestication. Given the opportunity, he will always choose to live in a herd or group and he still organizes his herd in much the same way as in the wild. During the gradual process of domestication, the sharp senses and good memory of the horse were used to human advantage. In addition, particular character traits have been selectively bred into certain breeds. Horse behaviour today is therefore a mix of nature (the responses and behaviours that are inherited, including those that have been bred into the horse) and nurture (what the individual horse has learned during his lifetime).

Horses learn mainly by conditioning – repeated experiences – of two main types: fear and reward. Both types of conditioning can produce the behaviour you want but their effects on your relationship with your horse are quite different. For example, a horse may learn to stand still when you are mounting if you hit him each time he moves. He will learn the behaviour you want out of fear of being hit. However, you can also teach him to stand still by rewarding him when he does what you want and ignoring him when he doesn't. By using this latter form of conditioned response, you will not break his trust in you and he will not learn to fear you, which may have unwanted consequences when you need to handle him in other situations.

As a horse progresses in his training, he learns new things increasingly quickly. For example, if you teach him to jump after he has got used to trotting and cantering with a rider on his back, it will be relatively easy for him. After all, jumping comes naturally to horses for escaping predators in

the wild. However, imagine what would happen if you got on his back for the first time and expected him to complete a round of jumps. With this in mind, the value of careful and progressive training is obvious.

Horse memory

Horses have a good memory and this is what makes them trainable. However, they can also remember things you'd rather they didn't. For example, if you have hurt them, they remember it. They cannot appreciate that you might have had a bad day at work and this was why you were grumpy. This is why everything that you do with your horse has to be "in the right mind." That it to say, if you are unavoidably angry or upset about someone or something else then stay away from your horse. It is definitely not the time to teach him something new and you could unintentionally create new problems for yourself and your horse.

Environment and behaviour

Domestication has, of course, changed the horse's living conditions – he is now largely captive and controlled for human convenience. For his own survival he has had to learn to communicate as best he can with his captors.

Wild behaviour

A horse learns many different types of behaviour – both good and bad – from his herd companions.

Unfortunately, the process of learning to communicate has in many cases led to the development of certain bad behaviours that have proved to "earn" him certain reactions that he wants or enjoys. For example, if he refuses to be caught in the field, the owner will go back and get a bucket with some food to try and entice him. He learns that if you refuse to be caught, you get food – so he just goes right on doing this because he likes food. Other bad behaviours probably result from the frustration of not being able to fulfill his natural instinct to roam and forage at will.

Recognizing your horse's moods

Regular observation of your horse, as described in Chapter 1, will soon key you into his moods and body language. This is essential if you aim to work with rather than against your horse – in fact, the latter approach is doomed to failure. There are some obvious signs that will tell you how he is feeling. For example, the ears tell us much. Ears pointing forward mean that he is pleased to see you and is alert and interested in what is happening. Many

HORSE MOODS

Fear
The ears pulled back and the whites of the eyes showing are clear indicators of fear in this horse.

Boredom and irrtation
The lowered ears and disengaged expression suggest that this horse is not happy with his situation. He may be bored with being in the stable and is beginning to get cross.

Happy and relaxed
With his ears pointing forward and a calm look in his eye, it is clear that this horse is comfortable and at ease in his surroundings.

horses have their ears naturally forward even when relaxed. Sometimes they will be forward but will be moving back and forth. This means the horse is listening to something that may or may not be a threat. When you are riding, such ear movements may mean that he is "listening" and trying to understand the signals that you are giving him.

When the horse is relaxed the ears will usually be angled forward but not erect. One ear might even be pointing back. When his ears both go back, it is a warning sign for you. He is telling you that he is displeased with you and may even be threatening to attack. Some horses will adopt this posture when you take their food in. This is to tell you not to steal their food. They will also maintain their dominance over other horses of a lower rank in the herd in this way, without actually making physical contact, such as biting or kicking. Herd order is thus maintained with facial expressions and body language rather than physical aggression. If his ears are held flat to his head and his eyes are glaring at you, this is probably the time to put the gate or the stable door between you and him and to reassess the situation!

Dejection

Horses also have a way of looking dejected when they are not well or are unhappy with their lives – for example, if a fellow herd-member is bullying them. Their ears and eyes seem to droop and the head is held lower than usual. A horse in pain may have his ears back but may also have them forward. His eyes will often appear to be staring and/or bulging. The look in his eye is very plain to see – he is frightened. This is the same look that he has if he is frightened by something, but this fright passes off as soon as the object of his fear disappears. With pain, the frightened look persists (see also Chapter 6).

Bad behaviour

Behaviour problems fall into two groups: those of handling and riding – for example, refusal to be caught or rearing – and other behaviours, known as equine stereotype behaviours, that usually develop in reaction to stresses that their owners place on them. These behaviours include cribbing, wind-sucking, box-walking, and weaving.

Difficult to catch

The best way of dealing with this common problem is through prevention by working with your horse from foalhood, if possible. Go to your youngster in

Bribery
A horse that is difficult to catch may need to learn that there are advantages to be gained by approaching a human in the field. This horse has been tempted to get close to his owner by the offer of a tasty snack.

Securely caught
Having succeeded in getting close to the horse, the next step is to attach a halter quickly.

the field several times a day. Pat him, talk to him and then walk away. Do this as often as you pass by. Curiosity will make him follow you either back to the gate or part of the way. When you do actually want to catch him he should come up to see what you have come for and be easily secured.

Difficulty in catching is a common problem with ponies when there is lots of grass around and they just want to stay and eat it. If a horse suddenly starts refusing to be caught and grass is not the obvious attraction, think about what you have been doing with him during the past few weeks. Have you been asking too much of him? Has he been engaged in some activity that might have caused him pain? Have you been angry with him when he did not understand why? If you think you may have upset him in some way, you will have to work hard to restore his confidence. Make sure that the cause of the upset – whether rough handling or exposure to some frightening stimulus is not repeated. Try to make sure all his experiences when you bring him out of the field are pleasant ones.

With any horse that is difficult to catch, it is a good idea to leave a halter (or headcollar) on while he is turned out. This will give you something to catch hold of if you can get near enough. For safety, choose a halter that will break if it gets caught on a fence or hedge. Alternatively, replace one of the joining rings with several loops of breakable twine tied in a secure knot.

One thing to avoid is bringing in his companions so that he will come in. He will just expect this all the time and you will have created a problem for yourself. You should also avoid letting him run into his stable loose. This will just reinforce the problem of catching him.

Refusing to load

Traveling to equestrian events is part of many horses' lives today. However, entering a trailer or horse van is a totally unnatural activity for your horse. He has to go up a slope into a dark place that resembles a cave in which a predator might be lurking. If he has been in a trailer before, he knows it will move around and be very noisy, maybe for several hours at a time. To go in at all indicates a high degree of trust. If your horse starts to refuse to load when previously he has been reasonably willing, then you should think back to the last journey. Perhaps another horse has bullied him in the confined space, or he has not had sufficient air when traveling or has been too hot or too cold or he has been uncomfortable in some other way. You will have to build his confidence again.

Protection when traveling
Always protect your horse's poll, legs, and tail in the trailer. He will also need a blanket.

Loading difficulties
A horse that dislikes going into a van, box, or trailer may become more reluctant to follow you if you lead from in front and turn to face him (left). Walking at his side (right) is more likely to produce a co-operative response.

Practicing putting him into the horse van or trailer and feeding him there will encourage him to go in. You can also try loading him with a willing horse (especially one that he knows), who will give him confidence. Always drive carefully with your horse's comfort in mind and try to ensure that every journey is a good one for him. In this way most horses will soon overcome their problems.

Biting and kicking

The horse's natural way of defending himself against other horses is through biting and kicking. There are very few horses indeed that bite and/or kick human beings without severe provocation. Sometimes a horse will aim a bite when being tacked up or when having a blanket put on. In most cases this is the result of his memory of a previous occasion when he was dealt with roughly and he is telling you to be careful. In time he may well forget his bad experience if you take care every time you carry out these tasks.

Asserting authority
Horses use biting and other aggressive forms of behaviour to assert their authority over other horses.

Some horses are just aggressive. If your horse is of this type, you will need to spend huge amounts of time just gaining his trust. When approaching an aggressive horse, you should always use a non-threatening posture, with your

eyes downcast and your shoulders rounded. Eye contact, raising the arms, or sudden movements of any kind could be interpreted by him as threatening (even if you do not mean to be) and will immediately elicit an aggressive response. Spend as much time as you can spare. Just sitting on a chair in his stable (perhaps reading a book) is a good way of getting him used to the idea that you are "safe." The sitting posture is non-threatening and you will not be looking your horse in the eye, which he may also interpret as challenging or aggressive.

Defending territory
Even in a stable some horses aggressively defend their space against incursions by other horses.

Spooking and shying

In the wild a horse needs to be constantly alert to the possible presence of predators that may be lurking unseen in the undergrowth. An unexpected movement or noise may be his first warning of an attack and his instinctive reaction will be to run away first and ask questions later! The domestic horse has not lost these self-protective instincts and, although most of the time he

Kicking
Kicking out with the hind legs is one of the horse's instinctive defensive responses against attack. This action can also be used aggressively to assert dominance over another member of the "herd."

Learning from mother
A foal can gain confidence by being regularly led alongside his mother. He will learn how to deal with new experiences from her responses to them.

Side-by-side
A horse that is nervous in traffic may find it reassuring to be ridden on the inside of a more steady companion.

will trust his rider not to lead him into danger, he may occasionally react to the unexpected by attempting to turn and flee.

Excessive nervousness most commonly occurs when a horse has not been sufficiently well educated as a youngster. Horses learn confidence from other horses in the herd – particularly their mothers. If the mare is calm, leading him alongside his mother on a regular basis will always help to give a foal confidence. He will learn from her responses to common objects and noises. When you start to ride him, going out with an older, more confident horse will encourage steadiness. Teach him to be calm in traffic by riding on the inside of an experienced, "traffic-proof" horse.

An older horse that has become sensitized to traffic – perhaps as a result of an accident or other frightening incident – is much more difficult to help. Putting him in a paddock alongside a busy road may help him to get used to the sight and sound of motor vehicles from a safe situation. Riding him, as you would a young horse, on the inside of a steady horse may help to give him back his confidence, too.

When your horse shies

At the first sign of nervousness as you approach a potentially "frightening" object, your first line of action is to talk confidently and soothingly. If you are riding, do not slacken the reins and pat him on the neck. Although this may seem like the natural thing to do, you are removing the supportive contact that the reins provide and you are also forfeiting control when you may need it most – for example, if he decides to take off. So talk to him, keep your legs on, and if you are with another more confident horse, allow that horse to go first. Your horse's instinct will be to follow the leader. If you are leading him and he is apprehensive of something, it can be helpful to take him up to the object and let him have a good look and a sniff, so that next time he meets it he will take no notice. This can also be done when riding, if it is safe to do so. Remember he learns through repetition, so the more often you can show him that the object of his fear is "safe," the more likely he is to lose his nervousness.

Rearing

Rearing is always an attempt to evade the rider's control. It can occur when the horse is being asked to do something that he does not want to do or something he is physically incapable of doing. This behaviour is rather like that of a small child having a tantrum. Rearing can be very frightening for a rider. While it is happening all you can do is lean forward and hang round the neck until he comes down. If you sense he is going to rear, you may be able to prevent it by driving him sharply forward and hope that this distracts him from

Taking the lead
A calm and confident rider will provide reassurance to her horse in potentially alarming situations such as heavy traffic.

what he was going to do. However, in the long term you will want to prevent matters from getting to this point. Try to work out what he is trying to avoid or what past experience he is reacting to and make sure it does not happen again. For example, if your horse rears going through gateways, he might have had a knock on a gate in the past and now remembers gateways as dangerous places. Start by leading him through, giving a treat when he walks slowly and quietly. Gradually work up to riding him through. Maybe you could put him in a field where he had to come through one gate to get into another part of the field. Repeatedly going back and forth through the gateway will cement this new confidence. Always try to discover what may have caused the problem behaviour and work out an appropriate re-education strategy accordingly.

Bucking and balking

Bucking, in which the horse puts his head down and kicks up his back legs, is an instinctive response designed to dislodge a predator that has leaped on his back. In a schooled horse it has many possible causes. Some horses buck because they have a "cold back." This is a term used to describe excessive

Rearing
This dangerous vice can be very alarming for an inexperienced rider. The priority is to keep your weight forward and to avoid pulling on the reins.

sensitivity of the back to the weight of the saddle and/or rider when first saddled or mounted. Sometimes the cause is discomfort from a badly fitting saddle, but in other cases no adequate explanation for a cold back can be found. Some horses just buck for the joy of being alive and others because of excitement when setting off on a ride. In some cases, a horse is actively trying to dislodge the rider.

Bucking can also be combined with balking (or napping), which is stopping in one place and refusing to go on. This form of evasion may be the result of tiredness or boredom on the part of the horse. He might sense a weak rider and decide that he has a good chance of winning a battle of wills. Alternatively, he might be in pain or ill. Of course, he might just be being plain difficult. The latter, however, is quite rare in horses.

There is usually a reason why a horse does not want to do something. As always, try to analyze what is going on in your horse's environment or routine. Consider if anything has changed for him, such as a new piece of

Bucking for joy
In the field a horse may buck out of sheer exuberance. However, bucking when a rider is in the saddle, is more likely to indicate anger or discomfort.

tack. If you think that he is in pain, you must find its source and do something about it. It may be something simple, for example, that his girth is too tight and you can loosen it. However, if the cause of discomfort is not obvious you may need to call your vet and get expert advice.

Equine stereotype behaviours

These behaviours are classed as vices and some actually cause harm to the horse. For this reason they have to be declared when a horse is sold. A horse that persistently catches hold of a door edge or other protrusion with its teeth (cribbing) and then uses this position to suck in air through his open mouth (wind-sucking) can give himself digestive disorders as well as damaging his teeth. Weaving, in which the horse sways from side to side, transferring his weight alternately to each front leg, will inevitably damage the joints. A horse that box-walks, constantly pacing his stable, uses up a great deal or physical and nervous energy and in a severe case may lose condition.

Cribbing
A horse who is in the habit of cribbing is also likely to wind-suck. Cribbing can damage teeth and wind-sucking can lead to attacks of colic.

Cribbing strap
The use of a special collar that prevents the horse swallowing air while his neck is arched, is sometimes effective for preventing cribbing and wind-sucking

There has been much research into these problems. The general opinion seems to be that highly strung horses (and this can include some ponies) that are kept stabled for long periods of time, especially when young, are at special risk of developing these behaviours. They may arise as a way of coping with the physical and psychological effects of boredom, frustration, and an inability to exercise their natural foraging instincts.

To avoid stereotype behaviour from becoming established, all young horses should be kept outside whenever possible. When weather or other conditions make stabling essential, young horses do very well in large open barns with others of their own size and age. There is also some evidence that feeding grain too early may predispose animals to these behaviours. Therefore a young horse should be fed on as natural a diet as possible. Between feeds of concentrates, make sure your stabled horse has a steady supply of a high-fiber feed such as hay. He can nibble this throughout the day to simulate the

Youthful high spirits
Young horses given the opportunity to run free and allowed to benefit from the stimulation of living in herd-like conditions are less likely to develop vices than those who spend long periods in stables.

A perfect match
You may be lucky enough to find a horse with whom you feel an affinity and who seems to feel the same way about you. This relationship is the foundation for success with your riding.

slow, constant feeding of natural grazing, providing something to occupy himself with as well as a balanced diet. The company of other horses is also a vital factor. One famous racehorse reduced his box-walking when provided with a companion sheep!

Getting professional help

Horses do not usually behave badly without reason. The careful owner looks at all the angles of the problem and works out a strategy for making it better for his horse next time. Keep in mind that your horse's behaviour is a product of every aspect of care and handling. A behaviour problem that you notice when riding may have its origins in some other aspect of your relationship. For this reason, it may be worthwhile learning the basics of techniques such as shiatsu and Tellington Touch that can be soothing for your horse and at the same time increase the understanding between you.

Never be afraid to get expert help if you are struggling. There are a number of experts, popularly known as horse whisperers, who work with the horse's natural instincts to resolve behaviour problems. They often produce sensational results with horses that were thought to be almost too difficult to bother with. If you consult such an expert, try to participate in or observe the session to enable you to learn some of the techniques and thereby replicate and sustain the good results after the expert has gone home. You may also wish to consult an alternative therapist. In many cases behavioural problems disappear after a professional chiropractic or shiatsu treatment. Herbal therapy or homeopathy can also produce dramatic improvements.

Recognizing a mismatch

Sometimes, when you have tried every strategy for remedying a persistent behaviour problem, you have to admit that there is just no possibility of a good relationship ever evolving between you and that horse. Just as there are some people in the world who you will never get on with, there are some horses with whom you will never make a good team: you will both be better off with different partners. If you do decide to sell your problem horse, be sure to explain the problems you have experienced to his new owners. It is only fair to the horse and his new owners that they start off knowing what to expect. It may be that what was a problem for you will not trouble them. There are many examples of great horse-human partnerships, where the horse has been a problem to every other handler and who just needed to find the right person for him.

Caring for a Sick Horse

Conserving energy
A horse that is sick often lies down more than usual. You will know what is normal for your horse.

Every responsible owner strives to keep her horse fit and healthy. However, despite these best efforts, every horse will fall ill from time to time. The unnatural environment in which many horses are kept contributes to susceptibility to disease, as does the mixing of horses from different localities, for example, at competitions and other events. A respiratory virus can quickly spread in this way.

Horses also have accidents both in general riding and in competition and also while turned out in the field. Ideally, the wise owner should make sure that her horse is seen – by herself or another responsible person – and carefully looked over at least twice a day. In practice what may happen is that the owner of a stabled horse sees her horse several times a day, while a horse out at grass may not be seen as often.

KEY SIGNS OF ILL HEALTH

Look out for the following key signs of ill health in your horse:

■ A visible injury that is, or has been bleeding.

■ Obvious lameness or painful walking for any reason, including reluctance to move; walking on the heels (as in laminitis, page 132), or groaning or flinching when moving.

■ Refusal of food. This means not eating his feed in the stable or if he is standing in the field looking uncomfortable and not grazing. This is not to be confused with simply standing around in the sun or just standing resting. Some horses will also stand and watch the gate when they are expecting to be fetched in and will not be grazing at this time. Look for a deviation from his normal behaviour pattern: some horses never eat up all their food and others have nothing at all left in the morning.

■ Variation from the normal in drinking habits. This may be a serious sign.

■ Looking uncomfortable and pawing at the ground, or repeatedly looking around at his flanks. This may indicate colic (see page 142).

■ Lying down for more than a couple of hours at a time. Lying down unexpectedly during the day or in the field (if he does not normally do this) can also be an indication of trouble. In most cases the horse will get up when approached. If he does not, but appears quite happy, then go back to him a little later and check him again. If he remains lying down and is not behaving as normal, get veterinary advice promptly.

■ Standing with his back hunched or his ears back or shivering. He may just have his back hunched and be shivering because he is cold. He may have his ears back because he is cross about something. Do eliminate these possible causes first.

■ Rapid breathing and/or high temperature. Groaning when breathing.

■ Dull staring coat. Sores or scabs in the coat or mane and tail. Any kind of skin rash.

■ A cough or discharge from the nose or eyes.

■ Loss of weight. Rapid loss of weight always requires prompt veterinary attention. Slower loss of weight also needs veterinary attention, but not so urgently.

Getting veterinary help

It is important to establish a working relationship with a vet long before your horse falls ill. Make sure his or her name and address and telephone numbers are at hand. A mobile telephone (cell phone) is very useful around horses. It means you can easily call the vet should an accident occur while out riding.

Calming an injured horse

The horse is a highly intelligent, very sensitive animal and, although we can use this to good effect when training him to do what we want him to, we also need to recognize our duty to help him when he is frightened. Generally, situations that may upset him, fall into two categories. First, there is the event or "thing" that he does not recognize and is therefore afraid of. A big, noisy truck passing him on the road or a new pile of building materials outside a familiar place would be good examples of this. Coping with this type of situation is discussed in Chapter 5.

The second category of situation that will frighten him is when he is injured in an accident. This can range from getting his tail caught in a bramble bush to very serious incidents such as road traffic accidents and broken limbs during exercise or competition.

In both of these cases, your horse is dependent on you for support. Nobody likes to see an animal hurt. If he has emerged from the situation frightened but unscathed, then all you need to do is to rub the area involved, talking in a soothing way and he will soon recover. Apply homeopathic Arnica lotion or give pills by mouth, as soon as possible. You should then take steps to ensure that he is not at risk again.

SERIOUS SYMPTOMS

Seek emergency veterinary advice if your horse has any of the following symptoms:
- Profuse bleeding.
- Inability to walk.
- Inability to get up when lying down.
- A temperature higher than 102°F (39°C).
- Heavy or laboured breathing that is not the result of exercise.
- Signs of severe pain, such as groaning, rolling eyes, difficulty moving, and sweating.
- Persistent signs of colic.

Immediate action

- Do not move the horse (except in the case of fever, see below).
- A horse with a raised temperature who is outside in cold weather must be brought indoors. If it is not possible to bring him into the stable immediately, cover him with a thick blanket. Once inside, if he is also wet, dry him off as soon as possible. This is best done first with towels and then by using a "wicking" blanket, which draws moisture away from the coat. Alternatively, if available, use a solarium or heat lamps.
- Ensure that your sick horse is warm enough but not too warm.
- Have a halter (or headcollar) and rope on him, because even if he is not moving now, he might jump up suddenly or attempt to run away at any time.
- If he is bleeding, keep him as still as possible. Bleeding can be controlled by firm pressure on the injury with a clean cloth.

Taking your horse's temperature
With someone holding your horse, insert a clinical thermometer into the anus. Leave for at least 30 seconds. The normal temperature for a healthy horse is 101–101.5°F (38.5°C).

Calm reassurance
After even a minor accident such as a fall, use your voice and the reassuring touch of your hand on his neck to let your horse know that all is well.

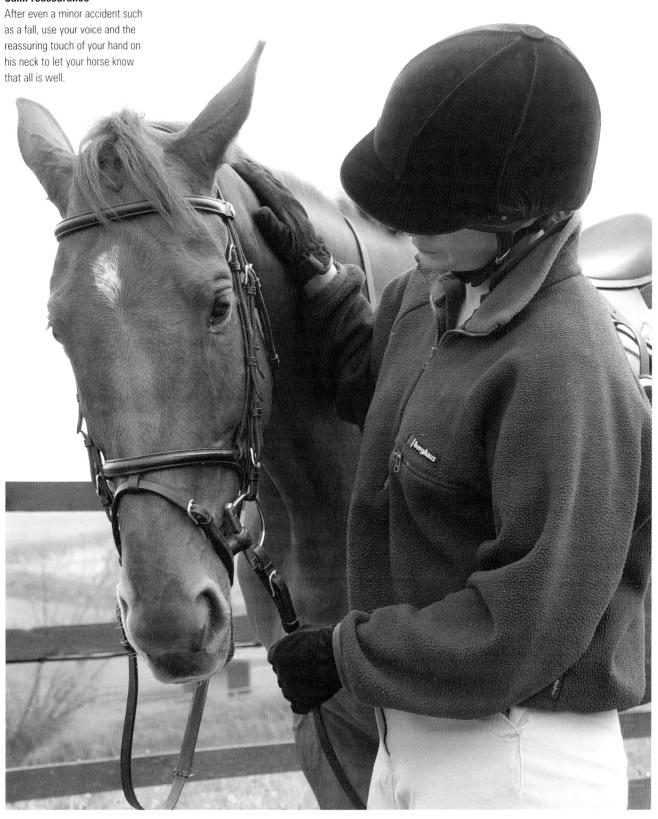

Dealing with injury

It is far more difficult to deal with a frightened horse when he is injured, partly because your own emotions are also involved. As you approach him, say an affirmation. Something like "I will be strong and calm and I will be able to help." Always use his name and keep repeating this to yourself. It is amazing what power affirmations have. Take several deep breaths and approach him calmly. Assess the problem as quickly as you can and if possible remove him from the source of the danger. If he is down on the ground, do not attempt to get him up quickly, you will just panic him more, and because horses are easily concussed, if you get him up too quickly, he may fall again. Crouch in the area of his head and neck, stroking him and talking, while you or a companion assess the damage. Your horse will get up when he is ready.

Immediate action

If you are not alone with your horse at the time of the accident, someone else should be sent to get veterinary help, while you, the familiar person, stay with him. If he is bleeding badly, you will need to use whatever is to hand to staunch the blood flow. It is always wise to have Rescue Remedy somewhere handy when working with horses. You should give him around ten drops just inside his bottom lip and repeat this at half hourly intervals. Take some yourself too, it will help to sustain you. A useful alternative to this is the homeopathic remedy Aconite.

Always keep a shocked horse warm. Putting on a thick blanket can often have a calming effect when a horse is stressed. Move him to his stable, as soon as circumstances allow. This is his special place and that too will help to relieve him. Add extra to his bed as soon as you can, so that he is completely comfortable. Horses can shake very badly when injured. If he is still shaking after you have put the blanket on, you should massage his ears and forehead, pulling his forelock very gently downwards. It can also give relief if you put your arm over his neck, which provides the same type of comforting contact as when a mare places her head over the foal's neck.

If you already have a close relationship with your horse, he is more likely to trust you to help him. If you are dealing with a horse that you do not know, the positive side is that there will be far less emotional involvement and therefore it will be easier for you to keep calm. In a tense situation, always remember to breathe deeply.

Following veterinary advice

It is vital that you follow your veterinarian's instructions to the letter. Make sure you ask for advice about feeding and exercise, and write it down at the time in case you forget later. If your horse has laminitis, for example, and the vet says do not put him in the field until he has seen him again, then do not think that because he is fretting and it is a nice day, you can put him out. This could have serious long-term consequences for your horse's well-being. Always remember to ask what changes in your horse's condition to look for and what action to take in this case.

Hygienic precautions

The stable in which you keep a sick horse must be kept especially clean. This means mucking out at least twice a day and providing plenty of clean bedding. Every dropping should be picked up, as soon as practicable. His water and feed buckets should be scrubbed inside and out, twice a day. For infectious conditions, blankets should be changed and laundered frequently using a good ecological detergent or nonallergenic laundry powder and you

Warm and comfortable
Unless the weather is particularly hot, a sick horse will in most cases benefit from a warm blanket. An extra layer of bedding provides added insulation if he wants to lie down.

YOUR EQUINE FIRST AID KIT

It is important to remember that the first aid kit is for "first aid." It should not include a collection of veterinary drugs left over from previous illnesses and kept just in case they are needed again. Old medications should always be discarded after treatment has ended, unless your vet specifically advises otherwise. Be sure to replace items that have been used as soon as possible, so that your kit is always complete when you need it again. Keep these items somewhere where they can be easily found, ideally in a clearly marked, clean, closed box. Your kit could include the following:

1. Cleansing agents for wounds. Proprietary veterinary solutions are shown, but tea tree wipes, which are now widely available, are a natural alternative.

2. Antiseptic cream (choose a standard veterinary product or one containing tea tree oil).

3. Leg bandages and padding.

4. Cotton wadding for making poultices.

5. Sterile wound dressings and gauze.

6. Clinical thermometer.

7. Scissors and tweezers.

8. Stethoscope (if you know how to use one).

9. Cold pack.

10. Antiseptic wound powder.

In addition you may like to include the following natural remedies:

▪ Lavender aromatherapy oil.

▪ Rescue Remedy.

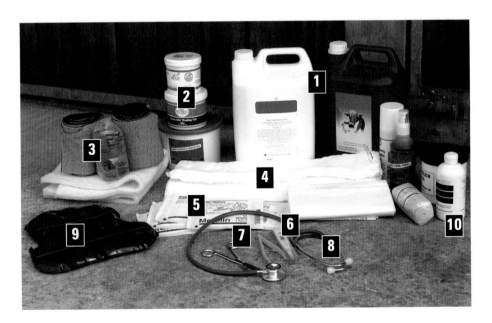

should wash your hands after handling the horse. If he is coughing or has a nasal discharge, then the walls and stable fittings should be regularly washed down with water. Air-drying and exposure to sunlight, plus the use of lime on the stable floor help to limit the spread of infection.

Spend as much time as possible with your sick horse. Grooming and massage are beneficial and keep his circulation moving. Just having you there can help some horses to cope better with their illness. If your horse has to be isolated from other horses (your vet will advise when this is necessary), human contact is even more important. If he gets stressed away from his companions, then a radio left playing while you are absent may help.

Feeding during sickness

Feed little and often and take away any food that remains uneaten after a few hours. Your sick horse will probably enjoy treats such as apples and carrots (preferably organic). Unless your horse is forbidden grass because of his condition you can cut long grass (from a clean source) and offer it to your horse. Grass can be positively beneficial in colic cases (see page 142).

Coping with serious illness

When your horse is seriously ill there can be an enormous emotional impact on you. However, you have to be strong for him. You are the one that will have to carry out his care and treatment. Spend as much time as you can with him. In some circumstances – for example, if he has suffered a serious injury – his condition may be so distressing that you can hardly bear to look at him. However, the more time you spend with him the more you will get used to his condition. Horses generally love you to be there when they are ill because it gives them reassurance. Yet there are cases when a sick horse wants to be left alone. He will show you this by laying his ears back and pulling a face at you when you enter the box and by possibly turning his back to you or not looking at you. Respect this but do ensure that you are there if he needs you. Do remember to look after yourself at this time. Caring for a sick animal can be very draining.

Practice some hands-on healing (see page 122). This can be done as often as needed. Be guided by your horse when he is seriously ill. If he likes you to groom him regularly then do it. This type of horse will probably also appreciate a massage. If on the other hand he seems to be annoyed by being groomed, then just do enough to keep him clean and tidy. This horse might

HEALING HANDS

When your horse is ill and distressed, you could try the following healing exercise. It requires no previous training or experience. The ability to give healing is something that we can all cultivate.

1. Wash your hands before you start. Put your hands on his back (there is no need to take the blanket off if it is needed). Put one hand behind the withers and one just in front of his pelvis. Spread your fingers out and close your eyes. You may need to tie him up if he is restless.

2. Breathe slowly and clear your mind of day-to-day concerns.

3. Think about your horse and imagine him well again. Picture him galloping and jumping or running free in the field or whatever is your familiar image of wellness in your horse.

4. If you are religious, this is the moment to ask your deity to heal your horse. Use your horse's name in your prayers. For those who do not have a particular religious leaning then repeat the affirmation – "[horse's name] will be well; all is well."

5. You may find that your horse becomes very relaxed. Do be careful that he does not fall over. If he is already lying down, he may want to get up.

6. End the healing session by stroking your hands gently along his back and then stroking both hands one after the other in the direction of his tail. Wash your hands after the healing.

appreciate some different sort of attention or company, such as you just sitting quietly in the corner of his stable reading a book. Try to listen to him and judge what course of action is best.

Dressings and bandages

Dressings should be changed according to the vet's instructions and soiled dressings should be properly disposed of. Do remember that if your horse has a bandage on one leg, he will also need a bandage on the other leg. This is because strain will be put on the "good" leg and, if it is not supported, it may fill with fluid, because of the extra work it is doing. Indeed, leg bandages on all legs can be very comforting for a horse, especially in cold weather. If he is feeling weak and wobbly they will offer him extra support. They will also give him protection if he is lying down a great deal.

Keep him moving

If your horse is lying down all of the time, and this is not because of an injury, then you should try to turn him at least once a day onto the other side. If he will let you then this is easiest accomplished by rolling him over onto his back and then just onto the other side. Do make sure you have plenty of room to avoid his flailing legs and that you have enough help. It is not a good idea for horses to lie down for any great length of time, because of the risk of compression of the major organs.

The role of complementary therapies

For many conditions, modern veterinary medicine provides the safest and most effective first line of treatment. However, complementary therapies can often provide a valuable supporting role, even in the case of serious illness or injury. In less serious conditions, complementary therapies can often be used without the need for conventional veterinary treatment. There are a vast range of natural therapies to choose from, and many remedies are available over-the-counter at feed merchants and tack shops, or may be obtained by mail order. For further information on individual therapies, refer to Chapter 8.

Bandaging the legs for comfort
Whether or not your horse is suffering from a condition affecting the legs, it is a good idea to put bandages on all four legs. This provides support at a time when he is likely to feel weaker than usual. Use a layer of foam or cotton wadding and secure with a firmly wrapped outer bandage.

Choosing a veterinary practitioner

Some horse owners have little choice in their selection of veterinary practitioner. You may live in a remote rural location where there is only one practitioner within a reasonable distance, or there may be only one horse specialist among the practitioners in your area. However, if there are alternatives available to you, and you are interested in pursuing natural solutions to your horse's health problems, it is important to try to select a practitioner who is sympathetic to these approaches. In all cases it is in your interest to build a relationship of trust between you and your vet, and feeling comfortable about sharing ideas on how best to deal with your horse's well-being is a integral part of this.

Combining conventional and natural treatments

Many conventionally qualified veterinarians have an interest in or experience of natural therapies, such as homeopathy and acupuncture, which they either use themselves or monitor the use of by a suitably qualified specialist. Ideally you will feel free to discuss the full range of treatment options with your vet and obtain his or her approval for any complementary treatments you would like to try on your horse. It may, however, be the case that your vet places little value on natural therapies and may even actively disapprove of them. This is a difficult situation that needs to be handled carefully. You must respect your vet's diagnostic skills and be able to trust his or her recommendations on the often necessary orthodox treatments he or she may prescribe.

If the condition is minor or if it is a long-term condition that is not immediately life-threatening, you may feel justified in trying natural therapies either alongside or as an alternative to orthodox treatments. The essential guidelines are that you first get a veterinary diagnosis for any unexplained symptoms and that you inform your vet of any home treatments – conventional or alternative – that you have tried or would like to try.

The role of alternative practitioners

There are important legal considerations to bear in mind regarding the administration of treatments to animals. In many countries the administration of treatments to horses may only be carried out by qualified veterinarians. For example, in some states in the US it is illegal for a person without veterinary qualifications to prescribe medicines (including herbs, essential oils, and homeopathic remedies) or to administer acupuncture to a horse. Manipulative therapies, such as physical therapy, chiropractic, osteopathy, and massage, may be administered by non-veterinary practitioners if that treatment has been prescribed and is supervised by a vet. Similar legal restrictions on the administration and supervision of complementary treatments apply in the UK.

These legal restrictions leave a gray area in which an individual owner can inform herself about natural remedies and alternative therapies and use them on her horse at her own risk. In some cases, herbs may be regarded as a nutritional supplement rather than a medicine. If you have health insurance for your horse, it would be wise to find out if there are any restrictions on the use of natural therapies within your policy.

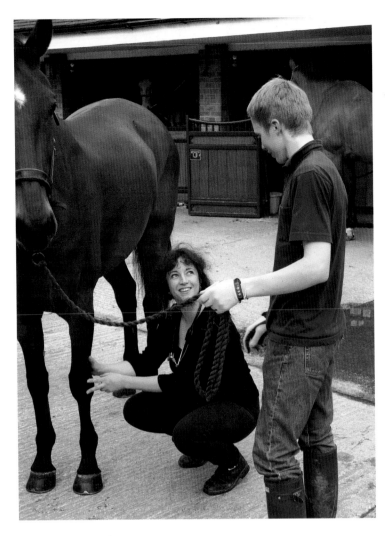

A relationship of trust
You and your horse will benefit if you are able to build up a good relationship with your vet that enables you to discuss problems and share ideas about suitable treatment strategies.

Taking the medicine
It may sometimes be necessary for your horse to receive conventional medications from your vet. This does not mean, however, that you cannot give natural therapies to support his recovery with your vet's agreement.

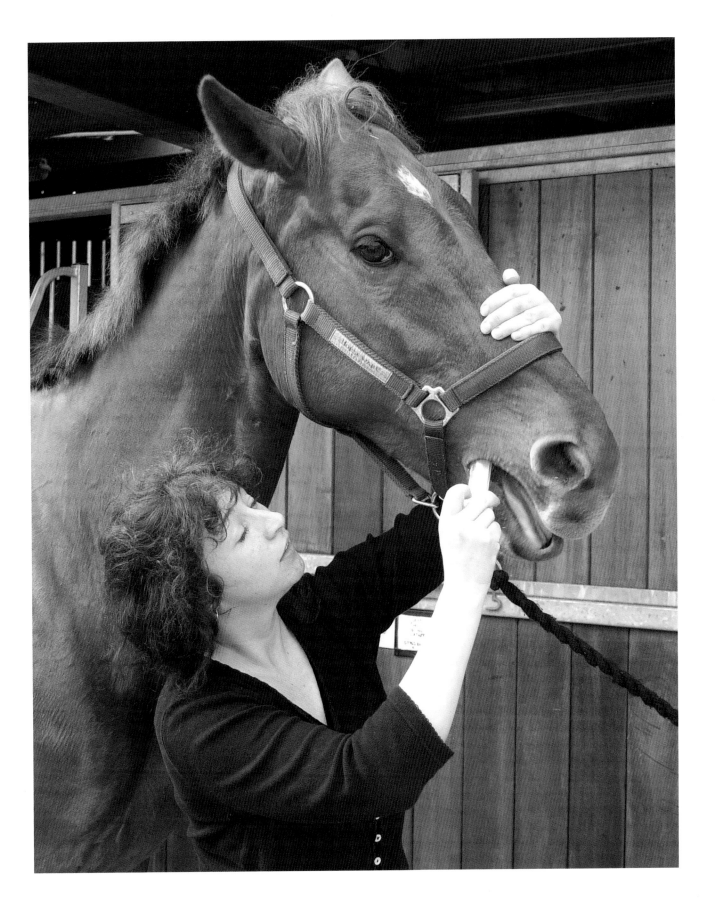

7

Common Ailments

*I*t is inevitable that your horse will suffer minor injuries and illnesses from time to time and you may be unfortunate enough to have to deal with a major health problem. This chapter aims to show how you can use natural therapies to support your horse's innate powers of self-healing. Sometimes these therapies can be used alone, in other cases they may be used alongside any conventional veterinary treatments that may be required.

What ailments are included?

The ailments covered in this section are therefore mainly those that are known to respond well to natural therapies. Other conditions, including some serious ailments, may also be helped by alternative therapies administered by an experienced vet, but because expert judgment is required, such conditions are not generally suitable for treatment by the owner, except under the guidance of a qualified veterinary practitioner.

INDEX OF AILMENTS

Using this chapter

The conditions are organized according to the symptoms they cause or the system they affect– for example, lameness or skin problems. Although each condition is described briefly, these descriptions should not be relied on for a firm diagnosis as many conditions have similar symptoms. It is important to obtain veterinary confirmation for any suspected ailment.

For each condition there is a listing of the natural remedies that have been shown to have been of specific benefit. You can select which of these you use according to convenience, availability, or preference. Generalized healing techniques, such as Reiki, can be used to aid recovery in any condition and are therefore not specifically recommended in every case. For further details and background information on the use of each therapy, including descriptions of herbs and other remedies, refer to Chapter 8, Alternative Therapies for Horses.

FRONT AND HIND LEG LAMENESS

Conditions that may affect either front or hind legs

Arthritis	130
Corns	141
Cracked heels	154
Filled legs	140
Foot infections	141
Laminitis	132

Conditions that mainly affect the front legs

Strain or injury to the front legs (including knee)

Navicular disease	140
Radial paralysis	136
Shoulder lameness	137
Sidebone	138
Splints	137
Suspensory ligament problems	136

Conditions that mainly affect the hind legs

Strain or injury to the hind legs (including stifle and hock)

Bone spavin	139
Stringhalt	138
Windgalls	139

Lameness and problems of the legs and feet

Lameness is probably the most common cause of veterinary calls to horses. The causes are many and varied, and sometimes the underlying cause may be hard to determine. Modern medicine offers a variety of scanning techniques to help in diagnosis, but even with such technology, the cause of lameness cases often remains difficult to pin down. A variety of natural therapies can help alleviate lameness, including massage and acupuncture. Refer to page 32 for further information about identifying lameness if you need help assessing this problem.

Arthritis

Arthritis, also known as degenerative joint disease, is a general term covering inflammation of the joints and consequent degenerative changes. Such changes include the wearing away of the layer of cartilaginous tissue that lines the joint and consequent growth of new bone. Carpitis is a form of arthritis specific to the knee joint and is usually caused by jarring from too much work on hard ground, especially jumping. Periostitis typically occurs in the pastern and is either caused by poor conformation

Common sites of arthritis
The joints most susceptible to arthritis are indicated here.

Hip

Stifle

Knee

Hock

Fetlock

Fetlock

Pastern

Pastern

or by too much work too early in life. Sesamoiditis involves the sesamoid bones at the back of the fetlock and may follow periostitis. Ringbone, another arthritic condition, affects the pastern and pedal bone.

If only one joint is affected by arthritis, trauma or repeated strain or jarring are the most likely causes. If several joints are affected, it is more likely that there is a more generalized cause. Early symptoms of arthritis in a joint are pain (manifested as lameness or reluctance to put weight on a joint) and heat. Stiffness in an arthritic joint usually eases with movement.

Orthodox veterinary treatment may include the injection of steroid drugs into the affected joint and/or the administration of anti-inflammatory painkilling drugs such as phenylbutazone.

Natural remedies

Herbal
■ Anti-inflammatory herbs such as dandelion, devil's claw, meadow-sweet, or willow given in the feed may be of benefit. Use a proprietary herbal preparation designed especially for horses.

Homeopathic
■ Apis 6c, when joints are swollen.
■ Rhus toxicodendron 30c, when lameness wears off during exercise.

Massage and physiotherapy
Both these forms of treatment can help to relax muscles that have become tense with pain and ease stiffness in affected joints.

Other remedies
■ Up to ⅓ pint (300 ml) daily of apple cider vinegar can help to ease joint inflammation. This can be given in the feed or in drinking water.
■ Chili oil, available from health-food stores for human use, rubbed into painful joints can also bring relief.

Too much of a good thing
Grazing that is too rich can lead to laminitis in susceptible animals. Ponies are at special risk.

Foundered hoof
If laminitis is untreated, the laminae become separated from the hoof wall and the pedal (coffin) bone rotates downward. This causes pressure on the sole. In extreme cases the bone may even protrude through the sole.

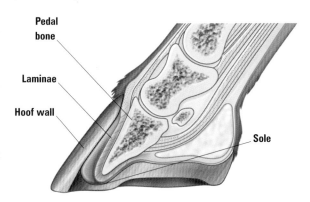

Pedal bone

Laminae

Hoof wall

Sole

Laminitis (including founder)

The scourge of the pony world and seen increasingly in horses, this condition involves disruption of the blood supply to the laminae, the sensitive tissues that line the inside of the hoof wall. If untreated, this can lead to damage to the internal structures of the hoof – a condition often known as founder (see left). The most usual cause of laminitis is overconsumption of carbohydrate, often by small ponies on lush spring grass. Grass grown today (especially if treated with artificial nitrogenous fertilizers) is just too "rich" for many pony breeds, who evolved to live on poor hill or mountain grazing. Excessive levels of carbohydrate disrupt the normal bacterial activity in the gut leading to a build up of toxins in the blood. Laminitis can also occur as a result of concussion from working too much on hard ground, infection, and as an allergic reaction to some drug treatments.

The first signs are usually seen in the forefeet. The pony is reluctant to move and when he does so walks with his feet out in front. He also stands in a typical laminitis position with the feet out in front and the weight taken on the back feet. In addition to lameness, particularly of the front legs, symptoms may include raised temperature and diarrhea. This condition requires immediate veterinary attention. The vet may need to be called at first to administer painkillers and possibly drugs to slow down the circulation and thus lessen the effect of blood collecting and pulsing in the feet which is very painful for the pony. Cold hosing can help to relieve the pain.

Treatment usually involves restriction of food intake, if excessively concentrated food is the cause. However, you should be careful of actually starving the horse. Follow your vet's advice on a suitable feeding regime. Gentle exercise on a soft surface should be started as soon as possible. Any horse or pony that has had laminitis, may be prone to it again and should be carefully watched. An experienced veterinary homeopath may be able to help to resolve the condition and lessen the tendency to recurrence with specific homeopathic remedies and dietary advice.

Laminitis stance
A horse who is suffering from laminitis may try to avoid pain in the sensitive laminae by taking his weight on his heels.

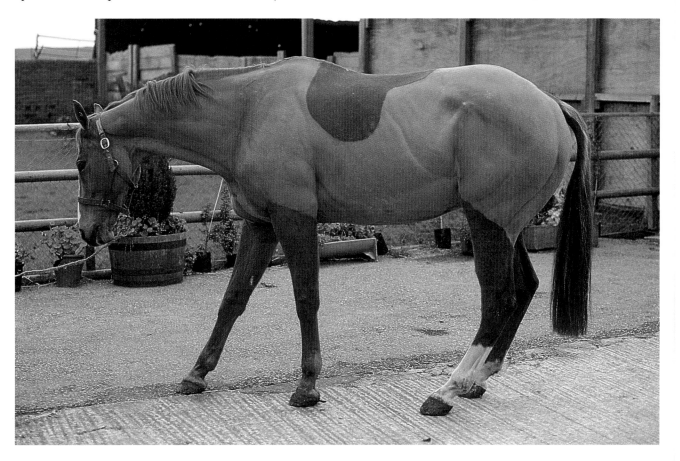

Herbal

- Dandelion, garlic, and nettle can help cleanse the blood.
- Milk thistle is beneficial for the liver, enhancing its ability to clear toxins from the blood.
- Devil's claw and cleavers are also useful.

Homeopathic

- Aconite 30c. This is the first treatment that should be given and should be repeated every 30 minutes for six doses. It can be combined with Belladonna 1M when the pulse is rapid and pounding.
- Calcarea fluorica 30c encourages the structures of the feet to return to normal if the problem was not too advanced before being spotted.
- Nux vomica 1M helps to clear the congestion in the circulatory system.

Massage

Horses with laminitis usually welcome a daily massage. It helps to restore the circulation to normal and relieves muscle tension that builds up when an animal is in pain.

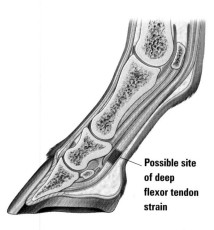

Possible site of deep flexor tendon strain

Sites of strain
The tendons in the lower leg are susceptible to strain. A common site is shown above.

Tendon injury

The tendons are the strong bands of fibrous tissue that connect muscle to bone. Injury is almost always the result of strain from overwork, such as can occur when a horse regularly competes in high-stress sports such as eventing or racing. The tendons can also be put under pressure if the spine is out of alignment or there is incorrect shoeing.

Damaged tendons need rest more than anything else for good recovery. Your horse should be confined to the stable. A cold compress may help to ease inflammation immediately after an injury and your vet may recommend immobilization of the affected area in a plaster cast. Once the injury has healed, a graduated program of exercise, including perhaps physiotherapy under the supervision of your vet, will help restore the normal functioning of the limb.

ASSESSING THE CAUSE OF LAMENESS

1 A vet will carry out a thorough examination. Farrier's pinchers are used to check for tenderness in the foot.

2 Gentle flexion of the fetlock joint may reveal stiffness in this area.

3 The vet may hold the knee flexed for a up to a minute and then ask for the horse to be trotted to check for joint lameness.

4 Shoulder lameness may be revealed by a reduced range of movement when the foreleg is lifted out in front.

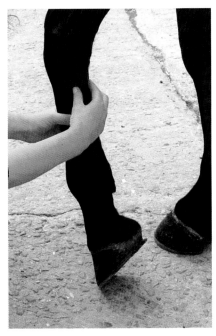

5 A check for abnormalities along the bones and tendons of the lower leg is an essential part of the examination.

6 Resting the fetlock on the knee permits a check for problems that are only noticeable when the tendons are fully relaxed.

Natural remedies

Herbal
■ Hawthorn may help to stimulate circulation to the injured part. See also Arthritis, page 130.

Homeopathic
■ Ruta graveolens 30c and Arnica 30c should be given as soon as possible following the injury.

Other therapies
■ Magnet therapy can help to speed healing. Special boots incorporating magnets are now available for horses.

Suspensory ligament problems

The suspensory ligament runs between the two splint bones at the back of the leg. It extends from the knee down the leg almost to the pastern where it divides, to rejoin at the middle of the pastern. This ligament is especially prone to injury in competition horses. Suspensory ligament strain is a condition that requires immediate veterinary assessment. Rest is an important part of the recovery process alongside any specific treatments your vet may recommend.

Natural remedies

See Tendon injury, page 134.

Suspensory ligament

Suspensory ligament
This important ligament connects the knee or hock joints to the fetlock and hoof.

Radial paralysis

The radial nerve serves several joints and muscles in the foreleg. A blow to the place where it crosses the humerus can result in foreleg lameness that may vary from slight to very serious. As with all forms of lameness, if you suspect this condition consult your vet.

Natural remedies

Homeopathic
■ Hypericum 30c.

Physical therapy

This can be particularly helpful provided you are certain that there is no fracture. Your vet will advise you.

Massage

Massage can help to keep the circulation flowing in the affected area and thereby speed recovery.

Shoulder lameness

Shoulder lameness can occur as a result of strain or injury. Occasionally it occurs as a consequence of a poorly fitting saddle. It can sometimes be hard to see if lameness is emanating from the shoulder. The best test is to hold the foreleg firmly and rock it back and forth gently. If the horse shows signs of pain or discomfort, then it is likely that this is where the problem lies. Consult your vet to confirm the diagnosis.

Natural remedies

Herbal

See Arthritis, page 130.

Homeopathic

- Arnica 30c at first sign of symptoms.
- Ruta graveolens may also be helpful.

Other therapies

Chiropractic, osteopathy, and physical therapy are often effective for shoulder lameness.

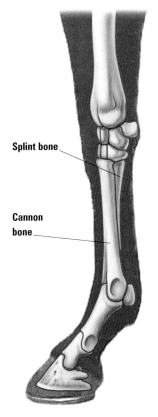

Splint bone

Cannon bone

Site of splints
Splints occur along the inside edge of the splint bone next to the cannon bone, usually on the inside of the leg.

Splints

A splint is a bony growth that forms on the inside edge of the splint bone between the splint bone and the cannon bone. It is the result of tearing of the ligaments between the bone that causes inflammation and eventually a bony growth. This may vary in size from that of a pea to a table-tennis ball. A splint causes lameness and heat when forming, but once formed and hardened does not affect the horse unless it is near enough to the knee to interfere with the action of that joint. It is usually caused by too much work in a young horse. Beware of proprietary products that claim to get rid of splints. They often contain strong chemicals and you may end up with no splint but white hair or, even worse, no hair at all on the affected area. Your vet may recommend laser treatment if the splint is troublesome.

Natural remedies

Herbal

■ Anti-inflammatory herbs such as devil's claw may help in the initial stages. See also Arthritis, page 130.

Homeopathic

■ Arnica 30c given as soon as any heat, swelling or lameness is noticed. Arnica liniment can be useful at this time.
■ Ruta graveolens 6c, four times a day to control inflammation.

Sidebone

This is a form of unsoundness most often seen in heavy horses. The lateral cartilage of the foot loses elasticity as a result of calcium deposits. Poor conformation can predispose to this problem, which is generally caused by excessive or inappropriate work, for example, on hard surfaces, or incorrect shoeing. Symptoms include lameness in one or both front legs, and/or heat and swelling around the affected foot.

Natural remedies

See Arthritis, page 130. A vet experienced in the practice of homeopathy may be able to recommend remedies specifically for your horse. Such treatment is often effective.

Stringhalt

This condition consists of an involuntary exaggerated flexion of the hock when walking. It can be slight or it can be extreme, with the leg being raised right up to the belly at each stride. The causes of stringhalt are unclear, but may be in part hereditary or may arise as a result of injury. This is a difficult if not impossible condition to alleviate

Acupuncture, massage, physical therapy, chiropractic, or osteopathy may improve the condition. Vibrational healing methods may also help. Every horse responds differently.

Bone spavin

An arthritic condition affecting the inside of the hock joint. There may be some swelling, but this is not always the case. Early symptoms may be a loss of impulsion in going forward and a reluctance to jump. Later the horse may appear lame in one hind leg, but often both are affected.

Natural remedies

See Arthritis, page 130.

Bog spavin

This is a swelling of the hock joint capsule, usually with fluid present. It does not usually cause lameness. Injury is almost always the cause, although poor conformation may contribute to the problem.

Natural remedies

Herbal
- Dandelion helps to eliminate excess fluid, if present.
See also Tendon injury, page 134, and windgalls below.

Windgalls

Windgalls are soft swellings around the fetlock joint capsule. Usually seen on the hind legs, they can also be present on the front legs. Although most often caused by too much work on hard ground, poor nutrition and adverse immune system reactions (for example, to a virus or after vaccination) can also be contributory factors to the development of windgalls. Windgalls are common in old horses and do not always cause lameness even when the swellings are large. If your horse is susceptible to this condition, avoid working on hard ground.

Herbal
- Garlic for blood cleansing.
- Dandelion to help get rid of excess fluid.
- Echinacea to boost the immune system.

Homeopathic
- Apis 30c hastens reabsorption of fluid.
- Arnica lotion to help to reduce inflammation.
- Kali bichromium 30c helps to stop fluid being released through the skin.

Other therapies
- The application of a kaolin-based paste to the affected area can help to reduce swelling.

Filled legs

Filled legs is a condition in which the legs from the knee or hock downward become swollen. It may occur when there is a sudden reduction in workload – for example, when bad weather prevents outdoor exercise. An old name for this condition, Monday morning disease, arose because it was common among cart horses who worked hard all week and rested on Sunday. By Monday their legs had become swollen.

The simple remedy for this condition is to get the horse moving again. To prevent recurrence of the condition it may be helpful to increase the amount of natural exercise – either by increasing the amount of turn-out time or by using a larger stable. Gentle exercise boosts the effciciency of the circulation, which reduces the accumulations of fluid in the limbs.

Navicular disease

The tiny navicular bone in the foot acts as a pulley for the deep flexor tendon, which passes over it. Navicular disease (sometimes known as navicular, for short) is degeneration of the navicular bone. The causes are not thoroughly understood, but it is known that some breeds (particularly warmblooded types) are more prone to this condition than others and stress from overwork may also play a role. Activities involving quick braking and

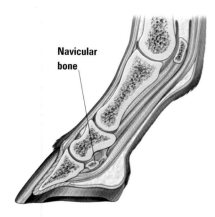

Navicular bone

Navicular bone
Degeneration of this small bone may be the result of repeated trauma and reduced blood supply.

turning seem to place a particular stress on this area. The main symptom
is lameness. An affected horse's gait may be altered and he may have a
tendency to trip. Correct shoeing is particularly important for a horse that
suffers from this condition. Your vet may recommend treatment with drugs
that maintain the blood supply to the navicular bone and thereby slow down
degeneration. Surgery to sever the nerves that supply the foot, thereby
relieving pain, is also sometimes advised. However, there are serious
drawbacks to such surgery: there is a risk that the horse will become less sure-
footed and may also be less sensitive to pain so that other hoof problems may
go unnoticed.

Natural remedies

See Arthritis, page 130. A vet experienced in the practice
of homeopathy may be able to recommend remedies
specifically for your horse. Such treatment is often effective.
Acupucture has produced good results in some cases.

Corns

Corns are bruises on the soles of the feet and are usually found in the back
part of the foot. They may be visible as a reddened area. There are many
possible causes, including badly fitting shoes, insufficiently frequent shoeing,
bad trimming of the feet, and working on stony ground. Rest and corrective
farriery are essential.

Natural remedies

Homeopathic
- Arnica 30c.
- Calcarea fluorica 30c.

Foot infections

The first sign of any infection in the foot is lameness with heat in the foot.
Similar symptoms can also be caused by laminitis, but this generally affects
both front or back feet and a foot infection is generally seen in only one foot.
When a foreign body gets into the foot and causes infection it inevitably leads
to inflammation. There may be no outward sign of anything having entered

THRUSH

This is a condition caused by neglect in which infection develops in the grooves (sulci) on either side of the frog. There is a foul-smelling, blackish discharge and the frog and surrounding area becomes soft and spongy. It is caused by prolonged standing in wet and dirty conditions – for example, in a stable that is not mucked out sufficiently frequently. Failure to pick out the hooves regularly can also contribute to the development of thrush.

Severe thrush requires veterinary attention. Treatment may involve cutting away infected tissue as well as antibiotics. The natural remedies recommended for other foot infections may also be used.

the foot, but the foot will be hot and sensitive to touch. Tapping on the sole will cause the horse to flinch. A conclusive diagnosis and treatment is best left to the vet, because he or she may need to open up the sole of the foot to release any pus.

Natural remedies

Herbal
- Garlic for its antibacterial and blood-cleansing properties.
- Devil's claw is also effective.

Homeopathic
- Arnica 30c may be given if there is a visible injury or bruising is present.
- Hepar sulpharis 6c or 200c is useful for any foot infection.
- Silica can help in cases of chronic foot inflammation.

Aromatherapy oils
- A solution of tea tree oil (10 drops to one pint of warm water) can be used to wash areas of localized infection.

Digestive disorders

The horse has a digestive system designed for browsing on relatively poor quality forage, taking in small amounts of feed more or less continuously throughout the day. Many domesticated horses have to adapt to widely spaced consisting of grains and other concentrated constituents that are not a natural element of a horse's diet. No wonder our horses are prone to a variety of digestive disorders.

Colic

Colic is one of the most frightening conditions that a horse owner can see. It occurs when the gut becomes distended as a result a build up of gas and/or blockage. Blockage may be caused by impacted fecal material or, in the most serious type of colic, by twisting of the gut. The causes vary and can include a sudden change in diet, stress, and damage to the gut resulting

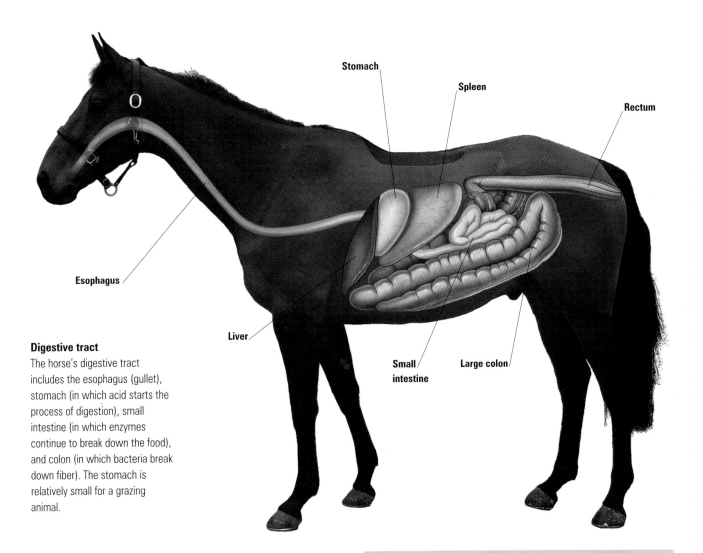

Stomach

Spleen

Rectum

Esophagus

Liver

Small intestine

Large colon

Digestive tract
The horse's digestive tract includes the esophagus (gullet), stomach (in which acid starts the process of digestion), small intestine (in which enzymes continue to break down the food), and colon (in which bacteria break down fiber). The stomach is relatively small for a grazing animal.

from worm infestation. Some horses who wind-suck (see page 108) develop mild spasmodic colic from swallowing too much air. Severe colic can lead to a build up of toxins in the gut and/or potentially fatal shock. Symptoms of colic can vary from a mild bellyache, which causes the horse to be uneasy and perhaps look at his flanks to a full blown twisted gut, in which the horse is clearly desperate and in extreme pain. Most cases fall in between the two. If the gut is twisted, urgent surgery is usually necessary. If the gut is blocked by fecal material, medicinal mineral oil administered by a tube into the horse's stomach may clear the blockage in the gut without the need for surgery.

KEY SYMPTOMS OF COLIC

Call your vet if you notice two or more of the following symptoms in your horse:

- Uneasiness and unusual restlessness.
- Breathing is faster than normal.
- Sweating at rest.
- Turning toward or kicking at the stomach.
- Unusually anxious expression.
- Raised temperature.
- Crouching or lying down.
- Pressing hindquarters against the wall.
- Attempting, without success, to urinate.
- Grunting, groaning, or sighing.

Rolling
A horse with colic may roll in distress. An owner who knows her horse well can usually distinguish this from rolling for pleasure.

Natural remedies

You can help to prevent colic by making sure that your horse receives plenty of fluid and fiber in the diet. If you suspect colic, seek immediate veterinary advice. Meanwhile walk your horse and allow him to nibble a little grass if he shows interest. Natural remedies can be used for colic prevention or in conjunction with veterinary treatment.

Herbal
■ Chamomile and valerian, which have a relaxant effect on the gut, can help relieve muscle spasm in the gut.
■ Mint is the best herb for colic-prone horses. A daily dose can help prevent build up of gases.
■ Marshmallow can also soothe the gut.

Homeopathic
■ Aconite 6c, can be effective in the early stages of any type of colic.

Aromatherapy oils
■ Jasmine or vetiver oils may help to prevent attacks of colic caused by wind-sucking.

Flower essences
■ Rescue Remedy. Administer four drops into the side of the mouth every half-hour at the first sign of colic.

Other therapies
Horses who are prone to colic attacks may well benefit from having regular calming treatment such as shiatsu or zero balancing.

TIP

One treatment that works well for a horse suffering from spasmodic colic is to take him for a ride in the van or trailer. The movement helps to encourage the gut to move. Seek veterinary advice if symptoms persist.

Intestinal parasites
Parasites are part of every horse's life. Foals can become infected through their mother's milk and adult horses acquire worm infestation through grazing on grass infected with worm lavae from the droppings of infested horses. Many different types of worm may infest a horse's gut and, while they generally do not create problems, an excessive infestation may present a risk to their health.

A horse with a heavy worm burden may lose condition and weight. The coat may be dull and staring. Sometimes the horse develops a pot belly and may be prone to repeated bouts of colic. In an extreme case, severe worm infestation can cause anemia and even death. However, it should be borne in mind that a horse can be infested with worms and appear in good condition.

Worming, with a proprietary preparation at regular intervals is important for most horses. How often this should be done is somewhat dependent on your circumstances. For horses kept at large establishments where they are turned out together, worming every six weeks is important. If only one or two horses are kept together and they are regularly moved to fresh grazing, to prevent reinfestation through eating worm-infected grass, they will need worming less often or sometimes not at all. If possible, remove

USING WORMING TREATMENTS

All worming preparations should be administered with feed to avoid adverse effects on your horse's gut. A probiotic (see page 53) given for a week before and after worming will also help maintain healthy bacterial activity in the gut. Daily administration of garlic, either raw or in powder form, also helps to keep the parasite population down and may reduce the frequency with which you need to worm your horse.

droppings from a small paddock on a daily basis. In larger areas, frequent rolling and harrowing may help. If you have a large field, dividing it into smaller areas so that you can rotate the grazing can also help to reduce the level of worm infestation.

Nutritional imbalances

Compound feeds are based on an average horse, living on average pasture and fed average hay. In most cases they provide adequate nutrition. However, where requirements are not standard, deficiencies may arise. For example, lack of calcium is thought to be the cause of developmental orthopedic disease in foals. In some areas, pasture is deficient in selenium. Selenium is vital for maintenance of normal muscle tissue. Lack of selenium can produce poor performance and sickly foals. Excess selenium, however, can also be dangerous. This is why it is important to know the quality of your pasture and hay and to ensure that any deficiency of essential nutrients is properly diagnosed and corrected.

Any older horse that fails to thrive even when fed on what appears to be a good diet should have a blood test to check if there are any specific elements lacking in his diet. An in-depth knowledge of horse nutrition takes many years to acquire. A novice owner should therefore always seek expert advice on an appropriate regime for her horse (see also pp. 50–55).

OBSERVING THE DROPPINGS

A vigilant owner should always be aware of changes in the colour or consistency of her horse's droppings. There may be a simple dietary explanation such as a change in feed. For example, a horse recently turned out into lush grass may produce loose, greenish droppings. Minor changes are not usually a cause for concern, but you should be alert for the following:

■ Watery droppings. This shows that water is not being absorbed by the gut and the horse is at risk from dehydration. Seek prompt veterinary advice.

■ Mucus-coated droppings. This may indicate inflammation of the bowel. Seek veterinary advice.

■ Droppings containing undigested fibrous material. This may indicate inadequate chewing, perhaps as a result of sorenesss in the mouth or tooth trouble. Seek veterinary advice.

■ Foul-smelling droppings.

Respiratory problems

The way that we keep horses today positively encourages respiratory problems. The typical domestic horse is confined for long periods of time in a dusty stable. He is fed largely on hay that, because of modern methods of baling, is riddled with dust and mold spores. He may be taken to shows and events where he mixes with large numbers of other horses and is exposed to many different types of microorganisms. His respiratory system has further demands placed on it when he is ridden, yet many owners do nothing to safeguard their horse's respiratory health.

Viral infections

Equine respiratory viruses fall into several categories. Perhaps the most common is equine influenza (flu). There are many different strains of equine flu and new ones are constantly arising. Such new variants are often the cause of flu epidemics. The symptoms include clear nasal discharge, cough, high temperature, and swollen glands in the throat area. A horse with flu appears generally unwell and often refuses to eat. He may shiver, even when wearing a blanket in a stable. The infection and its aftermath can last up to three months. In some cases, a secondary bacterial infection may develop, characterized by a thick, discoloured, and smelly nasal discharge. Young horses and old horses are at particular risk from secondary infections, which can sometimes prove fatal if not treated promptly.

In a busy stable or barn the virus can spread rapidly so it is vital that a horse diagnosed with equine influenza is separated from other horses so as to limit the spread of infection. The horse should be kept warm and strict precautions to prevent the spread of infection should be followed (see page 148). A horse that is suffering from flu or recovering from this illness should not be worked until all symptoms have subsided.

Equine herpes virus (rhinopneumonitis) is also fairly common and again can affect vaccinated horses because of the number of different strains. The symptoms are similar to those of equine influenza but the virus can also take a form in which neurological symptoms such as weakness in the hind legs and sometimes even facial paralysis also occur. This infection can cause abortion in a pregnant mare. Recovery after infection is often quite slow and, as with equine influenza, secondary bacterial infections can occur.

Nasal discharge
A runny nose is a clear indication of a respiratory infection.

Natural remedies

Herbal
- Garlic, aniseed, coltsfoot, marshmallow may be effective for a cough that results from secondary bacterial infection.

Homeopathic
- Aconite for fever.
- Belladonna should follow Aconite where there is a fast pulse and dilated pupils.
- Bryonia for a harsh dry cough.

A veterinary surgeon trained in homeopathy may prescribe a remedy specifically for your horse and, in its later stages may give a type of remedy especially for the condition, known as a nosode.

Aromatherapy oils
- A few drops each of solution of clary sage, eucalyptus, frankincense, and tea tree essential oils dissolved in a pint (500 ml) of water and sprayed around the stable may help to ease breathing.
- Tea tree oil can be used in solution – 10 drops in one pint (500 ml) of water – for cleaning equipment in a stable where one or more horses are affected by viral infections.

PREVENTING THE SPREAD OF INFECTION

Sensible precautions to prevent the spread of infection in a barn or stable include the following:

- Move an infected horse to a separate building or to a stable as far away from other horses as possible.
- Disinfect stables occupied by infected horses regularly.
- Items used by infected horses, such as the feed buckets and grooming kits, should be kept separate.
- Do not allow infected horses to leave their home stable.

Chronic obstructive pulmonary disease (COPD)

This allergic condition was formerly known as "heaves" or "broken wind." It is the equine equivalent of human asthma. The main symptom is that the horse coughs deeply from his chest when exposed to a potential allergen. COPD may be triggered by exposure to fungal spores in dusty hay or straw and is exacerbated by being confined to the stable for too long. A horse that is stabled much of the time is at most risk, especially if he is fed on hay and bedded on straw. This is because the exposure to fungal spores in such cases is higher than for a horse that is turned out most of the time.

The most effective way of controlling this condition is to reduce exposure to the allergy-causing substances. Put the horse onto dust-free bedding such as shavings, hemp, or paper. Wetting hay before feeding it to your horse may help to prevent the release of dust, although this is only effective while the hay remains damp. Wash down the stable regularly to keep it dust free.

A horse with COPD can remain free from symptoms and in general good health if kept in dust-free conditions, but he will always remain susceptible to a recurrence of the problem. You should therefore be prepared to maintain

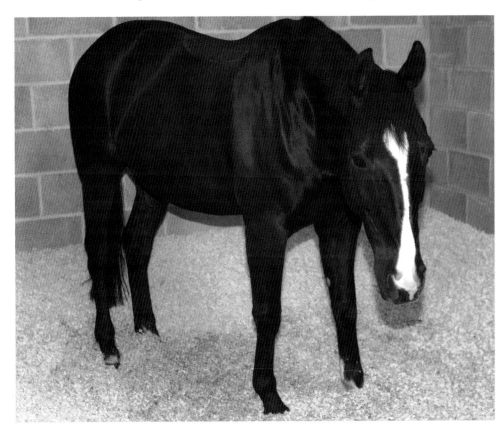

Low-allergenic bedding
A horse that is susceptible to COPD should avoid straw. Shavings are a convenient alternative.

his low-allergy lifestyle indefinitely. If possible, keep a horse affected by this condition outside for as long as the weather and the state of his general health allow.

Natural remedies

Acupucture
This has proved effective in dampening down the allergic response in some horses with COPD. Discuss the possibility of using this treatment option with your vet, who may be able to recommend a qualifed practitioner.

Herbal
See Viral infections, page 147.

Aromatherapy oils
- Add 10 drops each of clary sage, eucalyptus, and frankincense essential oils to a pint (500 ml) of water in a water sprayer. Spray the solution around the stable and onto the blankets of a horse who is susceptible to COPD.

Skin, coat, eyes, and teeth

The skin is the largest organ of the body. By keeping the skin clean and healthy, we can do much to help the general well-being of the horse. His eyes should be protected from fly-borne infections with a fly fringe or a natural fly repellent such as citronella oil. Care of the teeth is important too. The horse uses his teeth to shear off his food and then to grind it in a sideways motion. Any problem with the teeth will eventually lead to loss of condition.

Hives
In common with human beings, horses seem to have become more sensitive to the chemicals and other pollutants in the environment. The most common form of skin allergy is hives (urticaria). This produces raised patches known as wheals. In rare cases a horse may suffer additional symptoms such as diarrhea or respiratory problems. The condition can be caused by an allergy

to something the horse has eaten (a sudden flush of spring grass can bring up hives), by contact with external irritants, or by a reaction to an insect bit or sting. When a rash like this suddenly occurs, think about what has changed in the last 24 to 48 hours. It may be that you washed his blanket or his girth in a new, enzyme-containing laundry powder to which he is sensitive.

Underlying susceptibility to skin allergies may be an indication of abnormal immune function and vaccination can play a part in some horses. Normally wheals disappear within 24 hours without treatment once the trigger is removed. Seek veterinary advice if the condition persists or if there are additional symptoms.

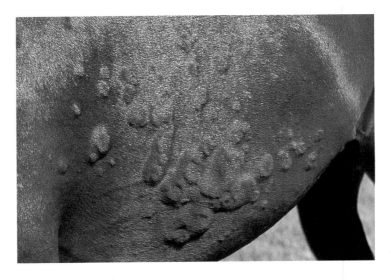

Wheals
The characteristic raised patches called wheals that are the main symptom of hives can look dramatic, but often disappear within hours.

Ringworm

A fungal infection, ringworm causes the hair in affected areas (often the head and neck) to become matted and then to fall out, leaving bare patches 1 to 2 inches (2.5–5 cm) in diameter. If the infection is unchecked, the patches may spread and join up to form larger areas.

Ringworm is highly contagious and can spread from horse to horse through direct contact or through contact with items, such as brushes and tack, that have been in contact with an infected animal. It can also affect humans. For these reasons close attention to hygiene is essential to limit its spread. Wear surgical gloves when handling an infected horse and do not share items of equipment with other horses. Wash brushes, tack, and other articles in a solution of 10 drops of tea tree oil to one pint (500 ml) of warm water.

Natural remedies

Aromatherapy oils
■ Apply oil or cream containing tea tree oil to the affected areas.

Lice infestation

This is a common problem in horses kept in large numbers without regular care or inspection. The tiny insects can easily become well established in

a thick winter coat. They can easily be seen by parting the coat and examining the skin beneath. The bites of these insects cause irritation that leads the horse to rub himself. Heavy infestation may cause a horse to lose condition. The shampooing method described below may help to discourage infestation, but you may need to seek your vet's advice regarding a more powerful chemical treatment.

Natural remedies

Aromatherapy oils

■ Bathe your horse using a shampoo to which you have added 10 drops of tea tree oil per tablespoon (15 ml).

Mange

Caused by several different types of mite, mange causes severe itching as the tiny creatures burrow under the skin. The horse is likely to rub the affected areas, which may lose their hair and become weeping and scabbed. Sarcoptic mange is most likely to affect the neck. Psoroptic mange is more likely to affect areas of thick hair near the tail or in the mane. If it occurs in the ears, it may cause head shaking. A third type, chiroptic mange is most likely in cold weather. It typically affects the fetlock area, which may lead an affected horse to stamp in an attempt to relieve the irritation. All cases of suspected mange should be seen by a vet, who will prescribe effective treatment, if the diagnosis is confirmed. Take appropriate measures to prevent the spread of infestation (see Ringworm, page 151).

Sweet itch

This is an allergy to the bite of the Cullcoides midge and horses who are prone to this are affected only in summer and early autumn. The mane and tail and surrounding areas are rubbed relentlessly in an attempt to get rid of the itching. Horses can end up with bald patches and sores that weep and may become infected, which further encourages the midges. It is important to reduce exposure to the midges, especially in the early evening and dawn, which are the worst times for biting. Special thin blankets can be bought that stop the midges getting to the horse's skin. Fly sprays and tags can be used and soothing preparations should be regularly applied to affected areas.

Natural remedies

Herbal

■ Make an infusion from nettle, rosemary, and calendula (a handful of each steeped in boiling water until cool). Pour this liquid over the affected areas to soothe itching. Add ice

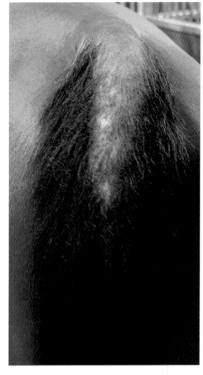

Tail rubbing
The irritation of sweet itch often leads to rubbing that causes hair loss at the base of the tail.

Herbal help
Regularly bathing areas affected by sweet itch with a soothing herbal infusion (see left) can provide relief from itching.

to the infusion if the horse is frantic from the itching.

■ Garlic in the feed is useful in cases of sweet itch for its insect-repellent properties and also for its blood-cleansing and cooling effect.

■ Apple cider vinegar added to the water bucket or feed also can have a soothing effect on itching and also helps to repel flies.

Homeopathic

■ Graphites can help some horses with this condition.

Aromatherapy oils

■ Oil of citronella makes a good fly repellent. Add 10 drops to about a pint (500 ml) of water and spray around the stable (not on the horse).

■ Mix the following essential oils: 10 drops lavender, 10 drops tea tree, 5 drops Roman chamomile, 5 drops yarrow, and 5 drops garlic (or the contents of three capsules) and add to approximately half a cup (120 ml) of aloe vera gel. Apply daily while the horse is affected. St John's wort oil (see page 179) can then be used to encourage hair regrowth.

Assessing the problem
Sores around mud-caked feet may go unnoticed unless you clean the feet regularly to allow a thorough check.

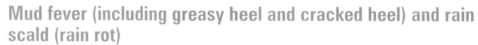

Mud fever (including greasy heel and cracked heel) and rain scald (rain rot)

These conditions are associated with continual wetting of the skin, which washes out the natural protective oils, and with chaffing from mud caked on the coat. These conditions allow the *Dermatophilus congolensis* bacterium to proliferate and penetrate the skin. The skin is reddened and the hair begins to fall out leaving scabby, inflamed patches. Any abrasion of the skin, for example, from ill-fitting tack or blankets, can allow the bacteria to penetrate and exacerbate the condition. In the case of mud fever, the area affected is the lower leg. The problem first manifests as reddened, sore areas around the hoof, known as greasy or cracked heel. Infection may cause the whole lower leg to become swollen and painful, and the horse is clearly lame.

Rain scald chiefly affects the skin of the back and neck and the horse may appear generally out of condition. Treatment is to keep the area dry and clean as much as possible – sometimes even keeping the horse stabled in bad cases until the infection subsides. Susceptible areas should be covered with a waterproof substance, such as petroleum jelly. If the sores appear infected, consult your vet.

Homeopathic
■ Arnica 30c when the condition is first noticed. Follow this with Aconitum napellus 6c if infection occurs.
■ Graphites may be useful if the area exudes a sticky, clear discharge.

Aromatherapy oils
■ Apply a solution of 10 drops of tea tree oil to 1 pint (500 ml) of warm water to affected areas. Or mix few drops each of tea tree oil and lavender oil into either aloe vera gel or petroleum jelly and apply to affected areas. Alternatively, apply a thin coating of a tea tree oil ointment from a pharmacy or health-food store to the area twice a day.

Other remedies
■ A poultice of slippery elm powder (available from health-food stores) will help to draw out infection. Lay a sheet of

Rain scald
The appearance of inflamed scabby areas on the back and/or neck can be an indication of rain scald.

cotton wadding on a clean surface. Spread a thin layer of slippery elm powder over the fabric. Soak with hot water and allow to cool to blood heat. Wring out excess water without allowing the gel that has formed to fall off. Apply to the affected area, either by bandaging onto the leg or by holding against the skin. Leave it in contact with the skin for about an hour or as long as is practicable.

■ Creams containing propolis, which is extracted from the material used by bees to make their hives, is a good treatment.

■ Aloe vera gel helps to soothe itching and encourages hair to regrow following infection.

Bruising

Brusing is a common consequence of minor injuries such as a kick from another horse or collision with an obstacle and is caused by leakage of blood from tiny blood vessels close to the surface of the skin. If larger blood vessels are damaged, a hematoma may result. A bruised area is swollen, tender, and warm. A hematoma produces a larger swelling that may be soft or firm depending on the area affected. Application of a cold compress or cold pack as soon as possible after the incident may reduce leakage of blood and swelling. Consult your vet if the injury was severe or if symptoms do not improve within a few days.

Natural remedies

Homeopathic

■ Apply Arnica gel or lotion to the site of the bruise or hematoma and give Arnica 30c tablets by mouth.

Wounds

Any open wound that does not stop bleeding after a short time or is deep enough to reveal underlying muscle or even bone, needs veterinary attention. So does any wound that is more than about three inches (7.5 cm) long (unless it is only a superficial graze) or which may have dirt or other material embedded in it. Any wound that appears to be infected (for example, if it is inflamed or exuding pus) should also be seen by a vet.

Wounds should be thoroughly cleaned with clean warm water and either salt solution or a proprietary wound-cleaning product. A solution of tea tree essential oil is also an effective antiseptic. Care should be taken to flush out as much dirt as possible, as long as this can be done without damaging the underlying tissue. A wound on a leg can be covered with a sterile dressing, if necessary, to keep it clean for the first day or two until a scab has formed.

TACK INJURIES

An injury caused by tack is a condition of which a horse owner should be ashamed. Such injuries are caused by dirty and/or ill-fitting saddles, girths, or bridles. The first sign of a problem is usually a ruffled coat when the item of tack is removed. If no action is taken, this may progress to hair loss in the problem area. Finally the skin may become abraded and open sores may be apparent. This is a serious welfare issue and any responsible owner should have addressed the problem well before it gets to this stage. Veterinary advice should be sought and the affected areas treated as for wounds (opposite). Do not ride the horse until the area is fully healed.

Prevention

■ Keep all tack clean and wash items such as fabric girths and saddle pads in an enzyme-free, soap-based laundry product.

■ Brush all areas that have been in contact with tack after you have ridden your horse and be on the look out for signs of trouble.

■ If you notice areas that seem to be rubbing, check the fit and condition of the tack (see also Chapter 3). Do not use the suspect item of tack until you are sure you have corrected the problem.

■ If you are not sure how to correct the problem, seek advice from a more experienced person or vet.

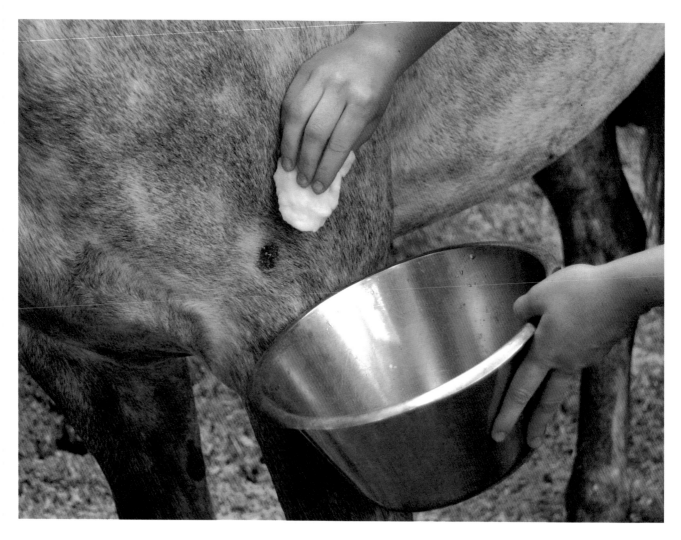

Cleaning a wound
For any injury in which the skin is broken, clean the area carefully. Be sure to use fresh water in a clean bowl and a clean cotton swab.

However, all wounds heal better when exposed to the air as long as there is no significant danger of further damage or of contamination that may cause it to become infected.

Natural remedies

For a serious wound, while waiting for the vet, administer Rescue Remedy immediately (see also pp. 116–118).

Herbal
■ Apply calendula cream or St John's wort oil both of which aid healing

Homeopathic
■ Arnica 30c. Give two doses, two hours apart.

- Calendula 6c helps to heal wounds.
- Hypericum 1M can be used for deep and painful wounds.

Eye problems

Probably the most common problem with horses is soreness around the eyes when flies are prevalent. This can be prevented by the use of a fly fringe attached to a halter (headcollar) to discourage the flies or by use of fly repellent. Serious infections, in which there is a thick discharge or swelling of the lids, always need veterinary treatment. Any other problem with the eye or any injury to the eye should be assessed by your vet.

Natural remedies

Herbal
- Make a soothing solution for bathing the eye from a teaspoonful of eyebright steeped in a cup of boiling water. Apply the strained solution when cool.

Homeopathic
- Euphrasia is a very good general help to the eye, whether for injuries or conjunctivitis.

Other remedies
- Minor infections can be bathed with cold tea or a teaspoonful of bicarbonate of soda in a cup of warm water.

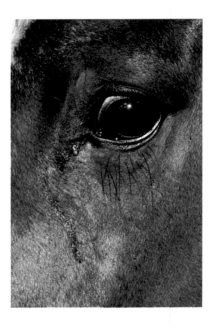

Runny eye
Discharge from the eye is one of the key indicators of infection.

Teeth problems

A horse's teeth continue to grow throughout life. Each tooth is worn away by the corresponding tooth in the other jaw and therefore keeps to a reasonable length. However, normal wear can sometimes result in sharp edges forming on the teeth, which can cause soreness in the mouth. This in turn can lead to ineffective chewing or poor appetite and consequent weight loss.

Regular dental checks and expert rasping of the teeth when necessary helps to avoid such problems. If a tooth is lost – for example, in an accident – the corresponding tooth in the other jaw will have to be rasped regularly to avoid problems resulting from overgrowth. Your vet should be able to recommend

Teeth and jaw
An adult horse has 12 incisors, 12 premolars, and 12 molars. There are up to four wolf teeth. Males and some mares also have a maximum of four canines.

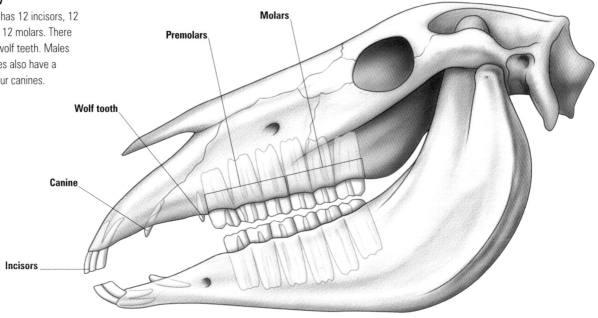

Molars

Premolars

Wolf tooth

Canine

Incisors

Parrot mouth
Normally the upper and lower incisors meet when the mouth is closed. When the upper incisors "overbite" the lower set, this is known as parrot mouth. Mild cases cause few problems but if the overbite is extreme it can cause trouble with eating and wearing a bit.

a reliable horse dentist in your area, if he or she is not qualified to do this work personally. Always beware of using an unqualified person to look after to your horse's teeth.

Bitting injuries
A bit that does not fit correctly can injure your horse's mouth, tongue, or teeth. Mouth injuries should be washed with warm, salt water. Change the bit and do not ride until the wound has completely healed. If a cut is deep, consult your vet, who may need to stitch the wound.

Miscellaneous general conditions

A number of equine conditions do not fit easily in any of the other sections are gathered together in this section. This includes generalized infections, cancers, and other serious ailments. There is no special connection between these problems neither do they have symptoms in common. These are all conditions that need to be diagnosed by your vet and for which conventional treatment methods are vital. However, in many of these conditions, alternative remedies and therapies, used alongside conventional treatments, can aid recovery or improve your horse's quality of life.

Anthrax

This is a comparatively widespread disease worldwide but almost unheard of in horses in the developed word. It is a bacterial infection, thought to live in the soil and possibly to be spread by flies. In horses the disease takes two forms. One is characterized by swellings primarily of the head and neck and the other shows a fever with abdominal pain. Both are fatal and the vet should be called at the first suspicion of the disease.

Tetanus

This is a disease that affects both domesticated animals and humans. It is spread in the manure of many different animals, and may cause life-threatening disease if infected material enters the bloodstream, for example, through a puncture wound. Symptoms include muscle stiffness and paralysis. Horse owners should therefore ensure that their own and their horse's protective vaccination course is up to date. An antitoxin can be given if a potentially tetanus infected wound occurs. There are no effective natural treatments for this condition.

Brucellosis

This infection caused by the *Brucella abortus* bacterium was formerly common among cattle and as a consequence also occurred in horses. Its virtual eradication from cattle populations has also made this disease rare among horses. The most common symptom of the infection in a horse is inflammation of the tissues surrounding the joints, especially those in the poll and withers. These areas of inflammation may become infected and there may be visible swellings that exude a thin yellow fluid – conditions sometimes called poll evil and fistulous withers. A firm diagnosis can only be made by the vet. However, after diagnosis, you can try a homeopathic nosode, Brucellosis melitensis nosode 30c, if your vet agrees.

Cancer and tumours

The most common tumours in horses are melanoma and sarcoid. Melanoma occurs most commonly in dark-skinned or gray horses, especially when they are old. It appears as small, round black lumps on the skin. They usually cause no trouble, unless they are in an area rubbed by the bridle or saddle

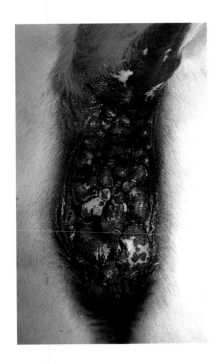

Melanoma
Most common in gray horses, this form of cancer usually manifests as clusters of black lumps in the skin, often around the anus.

or they grow together to form a large clump somewhere. No treatment is generally necessary. Sarcoid tumours are wart-like growths on the skin that may occur at the site of a previous infection or injury. They do not present a risk to general health but may be difficult to eradicate. Other forms of cancer are rare in horses and need expert veterinary treatment. However, any of the vibrational therapies (see page 191) may help your horse in his recovery, and will not interfere with an orthodox treatment your horse is receiving.

Cushing's disease

This condition results from excess production of hormones produced by the adrenal gland. It may be caused by a tumour of the pituitary or adrenal gland and often makes the sufferer prone to laminitis (see page 132). The symptoms are usually a loss of weight despite good appetite, an increased thirst, and a thickened and lengthened coat that tends to become curly. According to most experts, there is no successful treatment but the horse may continue to enjoy life for several years, only being humanely destroyed when symptoms begin to cause undue suffering. Treatment by homeopathic veterinary surgeons can in some cases produce significant relief of symptoms.

Azoturia (including tying up)

This is a condition in which the gluteal and lumbar muscles in the hindquarters become hard and painful during exercise. The common name for the disease, tying up, sums up the symptoms. The horse may become unable to move at all and may have to be transported home. The urine may be dark brown. The condition typically occurs in a hard-working horse returning to work after a few days rest. However, some horses seem prone to the condition and can get it at any time. Competition horses on a high-energy diet and an irregular work schedule are most susceptible. The condition used to be believed to be caused by a too rapid conversion of muscle glycogen to lactic acid, but now other factors such as diet and possible dehydration are also considered important. This condition requires veterinary attention. In most cases rest is essential, although in mild cases gentle exercise can be helpful. A change in diet may be recommended.

Natural remedies

Homeopathic
- Arnica 30c can be given in the early stages.
- Bryonia 30c can be given for continued difficulty moving.

Aromatherapy oils

■ Massage with a soothing essential oil such as lavender can be very helpful in getting the horse moving again. Be very gentle where muscles are in severe spasm.

Reproductive disorders

Most owners are attracted by the idea of their mare with a tiny foal running at her side. However, it must be remembered that foaling, although a natural process, is never without risk. When considering breeding from a mare, you need to bear in mind both her quality and that of the stallion so that you will have a good chance of breeding a high quality foal that will have a job in life.

Hormonal imbalances

This is a general category of conditions known to horse owners as marishness or coltishness. Both forms of imbalance manifest as excessive sexual behaviour. It is important to ascertain first whether this behaviour is caused by a hormonal problem or whether it is caused by another factor such as overfeeding, insufficient exercise, pain from a musculoskeletal, or other cause.

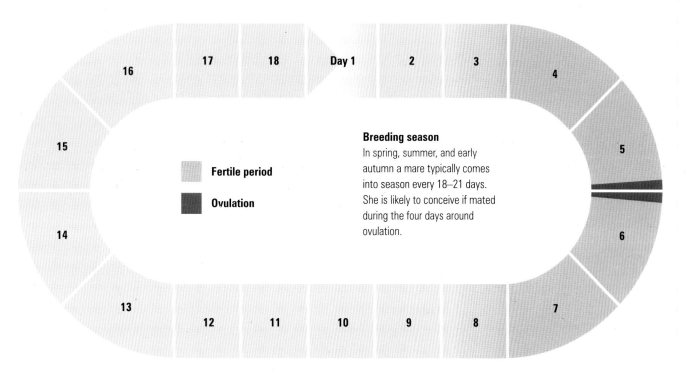

Fertile period

Ovulation

Breeding season
In spring, summer, and early autumn a mare typically comes into season every 18–21 days. She is likely to conceive if mated during the four days around ovulation.

Stallion behaviour
A stallion is often aggressive with other horses and usually needs to be kept separately. Some geldings may also show stallion-like behaviour.

For mares the symptoms of a hormonal imbalance, sometimes caused by ovarian cysts, show in exaggerated, irregular, or absent seasons. Some mares also experience altered behaviour while they are in season. For some this change may be slight, others show a marked difference. The mare may squeal or kick out especially when her back or flanks are touched and may be dangerous to handle. If your mare exhibits all or any of these symptoms it is best to get a formal diagnosis from your vet before you proceed to treat her with natural methods.

In most cases geldings are calmer and less aggressive than stallions. A gelding that shows stallion-like tendencies with other horses may have some testicular tissue left behind. This can be checked by blood test.

Natural remedies

Herbal
■ Calming herbs such as valerian can be used for both mares and geldings.

FOALING

1 The first sign that foaling is imminent is swelling of the udder. This may happen several days before labour starts or not until a few hours before. The quarters droop and the muscles around the pelvis slacken. If turned out, the mare tends to seek her own space away from her companions.

2 In the first stage of labour, the mare becomes increasingly uneasy. She may lie down and get up, and like a horse with colic, may kick at her belly.

3 As labour progresses, the periodic contractions of the uterus can be seen as movements of the belly. The amniotic sac (bag of waters) is visible at the vulval opening.

4 During the stage immediately preceding the birth the mare arches her back and may groan. The amniotic sac bursts and at this point the mare may take a rest.

5 Shortly after the front legs and muzzle of the foal appear. With a huge effort, the mare then delivers the rest of the foal.

6 After the birth, the umbilical cord may break spontaneously, or the mare chews through it. The placenta (afterbirth) is expelled a few minutes later. Once you have checked that all seems well, the mare and foal should be left in peace to get to know each other.

Natural remedies
Use the natural remedies as described under Abortion (page 166) for a normal labour.

When to get veterinary help
If you have never managed foaling before, you should discuss the process with your vet well before delivery. He or she will explain when a call out may be necessary. Don't hesitate to seek expert advice if you suspect something may be wrong.

■ Agnus castus and red clover are useful for a mare that has hormone-related behaviour problems.

Homeopathic

■ Apis 6c can be used for mares that have been diagnosed with ovarian cysts.

Shiatsu and massage

Both of these therapies can be used regularly especially for mares to help to regulate their systems.

Abortion

Abortion refers to the premature delivery of the foal, not to deliberate termination of the pregnancy. Such miscarriage is quite rare in horses and even more rare in ponies. There can be a number of causes including equine herpes infection and other infections, the trauma caused by an injury, deformity of the foal, the presence of twins, and colic. The signs are just as if the mare is to give birth but usually without milk being present in the udder. It is a traumatic event for both the horse and the owner and if the horse shows signs of very early labour then the vet should be called at once. It is unlikely that the foal will survive if it is more than four weeks early.

The mare should be treated very gently after delivery has taken place and everything done to minimize the emotional problems she will probably suffer. She should be back in the field as soon as possible and (if a ridden animal) be put back to work as soon as the vet judges it safe to do so. Be careful of putting her where she can see other mares and foals, which will certainly distress her.

Natural remedies

Homeopathic

■ Aconite 6c should be given at the first signs of labour and then every four hours.

Flower essences

■ Both horse and owner should take regular doses of Rescue Remedy throughout the labour.

The elderly horse

Many horses have a long and happy semi-retirement. A children's pony may be passed on to a new generation of children in the family, and while he may be too old to compete, he may be happy taking a small child for her early lessons on the lead rein or in the paddock. Some old ponies act as a companion and a nanny to younger ones, thus making them a valuable contributor to the life of the stables. Young horses that do not live in a natural herd situation cannot easily learn from their elders as they would in the wild. An older horse in the stable can teach them a great deal and may provide a steadying influence. What is important for an old horse is that he is not just stuck in a field somewhere and left. To enjoy a happy and healthy retirement, every horse needs some job in life. He needs some routine and some order to his days. Every old horse knows exactly what is going on in the stable or barn. They know feed times and the routine better than you do. If you forget to do things in the right order, they soon let you know.

Retirement

So when should you stop riding your horse? The answer is when he no longer enjoys being ridden or when he has a condition that causes him pain or discomfort. Some old horses may continue to benefit from regular gentle exercise, such as those with general stiffness. Those with a condition such as advanced chronic obstructive pulmonary disease may find even gentle work too taxing. Discuss these issues with your vet and use your instincts. Never push an old horse too far.

Death

The death of a loved animal is always distressing and the added complications of coping with such a large body as that of a horse can make things worse. Sometimes death happens gently, as for example, the old horse found dead under its favourite tree. Sometimes it happens suddenly, such as in an accident or a bad bout of colic. Most often, however, death happens over a long period of deterioration and aging, which will inevitably result in you, the owner, having to make a decision to put the horse to sleep.

You will need to confront the decision to have your horse put down if he has a serious chronic illness that takes a turn for the worse. Sometimes in such cases a horse contracts an acute infection and does not have the resources to fight it. However, usually the decision has to come over a number of days and weeks. If you are close to your horse, then usually you will just know when he has had enough. You will look at him one day and he will look back with no light left in his eyes.

When to let go

Sometimes the vet will help you make the decision, but if that is not the case, what are the signs that old age has become too much for your friend to bear? The following are good indicators that your horse may need to be put down.

- He has lost condition so badly that despite good food he is just not recovering.
- He is clearly in pain that is not controlled by painkilling medication – or it is so bad that it is controlled only by enormous doses.
- He has stopped eating, but does not have a problem with his mouth.
- If he cannot get up and down reasonably easily.

The practicalities

Book the vet at least 24 hours ahead, but not longer as you will simply give yourself days of agony. Make full use of Rescue Remedy for yourself and the horse, but try not to alarm him too much. There are basically two humane methods: shooting or lethal injection. Shooting is very quick and the horse knows nothing about it. However, it can seem very brutal to inflict such a wound on your beloved companion. Injection is slower but more gentle. Sometimes, however, the horse can go down and then get up again, which can be distressing for all concerned. Discuss the issue fully with your vet and accept that this is not going to be an easy day for you and you are just going to have to be strong for him. Make sure you have some moral support from family and friends later.

The body is something that has to be addressed. It may be an option to have him buried on your land. If not, you have to have the body collected for disposal or cremation. Your vet will provide full advice.

Living on

Your memories of your horse friend will never die. You will have photographs and maybe videos. You might have trophies, ribbons, and rosettes, or even press cuttings. You might like to donate a trophy to a local show or send a donation to a charity in his name, but whatever you do, his spirit will live on in your heart forever.

8

Alternative Therapies
for Horses

*I*n recent years, there has been a resurgence of interest in alternative and natural therapies among horse owners. Many such treatments have been in use for thousands of years, but with the coming of modern antibacterial drugs and antibiotics, these traditional methods of treating horses came to be seen as old-fashioned and were perceived as less effective. Most owners changed from using unqualified, but probably very experienced, local horse healers to using the services of a qualified veterinary surgeon.

This change in the emphasis of veterinary practice more or less coincided with the shift from the horse being primarily a work animal to its being used mainly for leisure and sport. At the start of the 21st century horse ownership for leisure use has reached an all-time high, and alternative therapies for horses have once again become fashionable. However, the fact that these therapies are seen as fashionable should not detract from the fact that they are mostly well tried and tested and many excellent results have been achieved. Alternative therapies sometimes offer a cost advantage in

INDEX OF THERAPIES

The therapies described in this chapter are organized in three groups: medicinal, hands-on, and vibrational healing therapies.

comparison with standard veterinary fees. But most importantly the use of natural therapies can offer gentle but effective treatment for a wide variety of conditions without the risk of potentially harmful side effects.

In this chapter the theory and principles underlying each of these therapies is explained, along with any relevant cautions regarding their use.

Medicinal therapies

Although there is a widespread perception that veterinary medicines are the only "proper" cures for ailments, an increasing band of horse owners know that herbal and homeopathic medicines are strong and effective treatments. In this book the term medicinal therapies is used to describe those in which a substance is used for its healing benefits. This includes substances that are administered by mouth and also those that are inhaled or absorbed through the skin. Follow the instructions in the text for the safe administration of each type of "medicine."

Herbal medicine

In the wild, horses used to practice their own form of herbal medicine. When pasture was kept as grazing for many years, and was fertilized naturally, all kinds of wild plants grew among the grass. As horses roamed free, they could use their instinct to find the plants that they needed to relieve whatever condition they were suffering from. When humans started to cultivate the land, no artificial weedkillers or fertilizers were used and the wild plants still flourished. Herbal medicine was also the medicine of choice (and availability) for their human keepers. So horse owners used the herbs that they used for themselves to minister to their horses. Herbal medicine fell from favour when new veterinary drugs became available. Nowadays, increasing numbers of people are realizing that herbs are effective medicines and can be particularly beneficial for chronic complaints such as arthritis. However, because herbs can have such a powerful effect, always consult your vet before using herbs or herbal medicines if your horse has been prescribed veterinary drugs.

If you are considering using herbs to treat your horse, you need to be absolutely sure of the identification of the herb and, of course, herbs must not be plundered from the wild. Some herbs can be poisonous or even fatal

Using dried herbs
Adding dried herbs to your horse's feed is an easy way to use them.

A welcome treat
Herbs can be given fresh if available and the fact that the horse relishes them is an indication of his need.

if wrongly used. Be sure to get sound advice. There are, however, a number of herbs an amateur can use for treating minor complaints, which are relatively easily identified and which can be used with confidence.

Giving herbs to your horse

You can use fresh or dried herbs. If using fresh herbs, use only those picked from a clean source – for example, away from the road or other possibly polluted areas. Discard any leaves that are not eaten straight away. A horse will often reject herbs he doesn't need.

Dried herbs may be obtained from health-food stores and there are a number of mail order companies that supply herbal products especially for horses. Alternatively, you can dry herbs that you have grown yourself.

Giving herbs by mouth

The normal amount of a fresh herb is a small handful twice a day. However, this may vary according to the herb, so check the advice given for individual herbs. The normal dose of a dried herb is about ⅔ oz (20 g) twice a day in the feed.

Infusions and decoctions

Herbal infusions or decoctions can be used to bathe a variety of skin conditions. The liquid can also be given to your horse by mouth in a large syringe or added to the feed. An infusion can be made with either fresh or dried leaves. Use about 1 ½ oz (40 g) of fresh herbs or ⅔ oz (20 g) of dried herbs per pint (500 ml) of water. Place the herbs in a container and pour over boiling water. Allow to cool and then strain the infusion before use. If the herbal material is in the form of bark or seeds, simmer 1 oz (30 g) of the herb in 1 ½ pints (750 ml) of water for 15 minutes, allow to cool and strain as for an infusion.

Key herbs

Dandelion (*Taraxacum officinale*)

If possible, all horse owners should grow a few dandelions in a corner of the garden for their horses. Every horse can benefit from a dandelion leaves every day and it is easy to dry them fo use. Sick horses will sometimes eat fresh dandelion lea when they will eat nothing else, possibly because their tells them that they need the action of this plant.

Dandelion leaves are a rich source of potassium and tl diuretic (water-eliminating) action can be very useful in laminitis. Their tonic action on the liver and digestive system makes them valuable in many conditions, but primarily laminitis, arthritis, and skin problems.

Dandelion

Devil's claw (*Harpagophytum procumbens*)

Devil's claw is often a constituent of herbal compounds that are sold for relieving pain and inflammation, for example, in foot infections. Although the effect of these remedies may take several days or even weeks to show, they tend to have fewer side effects than conventional anti-inflammatory drugs. This herb should not be given to pregnant mares and it should not be used with painkillers prescribed by your vet or with willow.

Garlic (*Allium sativum*)

Many horse owners know and use garlic, yet are puzzled by the fact that it does not naturally grow in horse pasture and therefore could not be sought out by horses in the wild. The answer to this is that ramsons, or wild garlic

Garlic

PROPRIETARY HERBAL MEDICINES

Do not expect miracle cures from proprietary products. Such products generally use only the safest and mildest herbs and, although they may produce good results, effective prescribing demands proper knowledge of the horse and the medication needs to be tailored to his needs. Always consult a vet if you are unsure whether a particular herbal product is suitable for your horse.

(*Allium ursinum*), grows in damp pastures. This plant is relished by horses and, although milder in flavour than culinary garlic, is nevertheless effective in similar ways. Garlic works as an expectorant (loosening mucus), an antibacterial, an antihistamine, and an antiparasitic. Human research shows that it helps to reduce blood pressure, making it potentially useful for horses that suffer from laminitis. Garlic also has a blood-cleansing action that is also beneficial in laminitis and in any condition where infection is present. Many horse owners give garlic routinely as a preventive measure and this has the effect of building up blood levels of the volatile compounds. These are excreted through the skin and help to repel flies. Garlic can be fed at the rate of five fresh cloves per day or according to the instructions on a proprietary preparation.

Kelp, seaweed

If you are lucky enough to live near a clean beach, then you will be able to collect seaweed for your horse to supplement his diet. *Fucus vesiculosus* is the variety to look for. It is commonly known as bladderwrack and is identified by the small round "bladders" along the fronds that pop when squeezed.

Seaweed is rich in minerals but also absorbs any heavy metals that are present in the environment, which is why you must be sure of your source. If you have any doubt, for the health and safety of your horse, purchase powder from a reputable stockist. A normal dose is a small handful of fresh seaweed a day or about 1 oz (30 g) of dried or powdered seaweed.

Seaweed is possibly the best coat conditioner and is thought to speed up shedding of the winter coat. This is a result of its iodine content. Certainly show horses who are given seaweed supplements do seem to develop a good bloom to their coat and dark colours such as chestnut and bay seem to get an extra sheen.

Horses that have arthritis or rheumatism can benefit from the addition of seaweed to their diet, as can horses whose grazing is thought to be mineral deficient. However, it can have a diuretic effect, increasing urine production, and caution should be used if administering this remedy to a horse with Cushing's disease, in which excessive thirst and increased urination occur.

Marigold (*Calendula officinalis*)

This is the traditional culinary herb pot marigold, not the French marigold of formal garden displays. It is easily grown in most gardens and its cheerful yellow and orange flowers brighten up the dullest day. The crushed petals have antifungal, antibacterial, and anti-inflammatory properties and are very useful for cleaning and encouraging healing of wounds.

Calendula cream is widely available from pharmacies and is useful both for application to wounds and to soften and remove the scabs of mud fever.

Marigold

Mint (*Mentha piperata*, or *Mentha spicata*)

Mint is very easy to grow in the garden – in fact too easy sometimes! Both varieties piperata (peppermint) and spicata (spearmint) are suitable for feeding to horses. Mint can be sprinkled on the feed of a sick horse or a fussy feeder. It relaxes the muscles of the digestive tract and can be given in cases of mild colic and, at times of stress, to a horse that is prone to colic – such as before or during traveling or competing. Fresh mint is always better than dried mint because the activity of the volatile oils is greatly diminished by drying. They relieve itching, a mint leaf can be rubbed on insect bites and also rubbed gently onto sweet itch areas where the skin is not broken.

Mint

Stinging nettle (*Urtica dioica*)

Stinging nettles are found everywhere – and are very good for horses. Yet paradoxically most horses in the wild or turned out do not choose to eat them. Many horses will take fresh nettles readily if they are cut down and allowed to wilt a little. However, some horses will only accept them if they are dried and mixed with the feed. Be sure to gather nettles from a clean source and wear gloves for your own protection.

Nettles are a good spring tonic both for humans and for horses. They are high in vitamin C and iron. A strong infusion (as many leaves as will fit in a jug when squashed down and covered with boiling water) left to go cold for 24 hours and then strained, can be poured over problem areas of the coat to improve skin and coat condition. Such a decoction is also soothing when poured over areas affected by sweet itch.

MAKING POULTICE USING HERBS

A poultice is a good way of applying herbs externally, for example, to treat inflammation or swelling.

1 Spread a layer of fresh or dried herb over a 12 inch (30 cm) square of cotton wadding.

2 Soak with boiling water and leave until cool enough to handle.

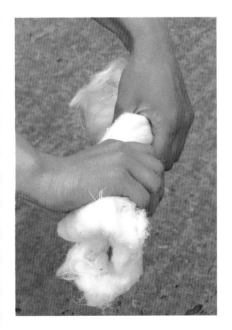

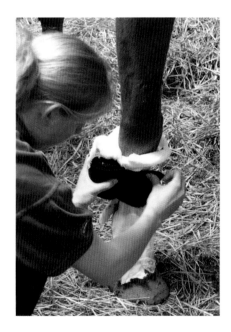

3 Carefully squeeze out excess liquid without allowing the herb to fall out.

4 Apply to the affected area.

5 In the case of a leg, secure with a bandage.

St John's wort

St John's wort (*Hypericum perforatum*)
The oil from this plant, available from health-food stores, is very useful for stimulating wound healing. It can also be massaged into inflamed joints and tendons. If the oil is purchased in undiluted form, it should be diluted at the rate of five drops to five teaspoons of a suitable (almond or sunflower) carrier oil.

Valerian (*Valeriana officinalis*)
Usually bought as a dried product, valerian has powerful tranquilizing properties and is nearly always a constituent of sedative mixtures. It is particularly useful for soothing agitation in colic or for mares with hormone imbalances. It combines well with other calming herbs such as skullcap and chamomile and does not have the hangover effect of veterinary tranquilizers. However, it should be borne in mind that this is a powerful herb and care should be taken not to exceed the dose recommended by the manufacturer of any proprietary product you are using.

Yarrow (*Achillea millefolium*)
A common weed in pastures in Great Britain and North America, its Latin name relates to the Greek god Achilles who, according to myth, used the leaves to stop bleeding on the battlefield. A handful of yarrow leaves applied to a bleeding wound is a very effective first aid measure and usually stops bleeding very quickly. It can also be used in the form of an essential oil (see Aromatherapy, page 187). Obviously, where bleeding is profuse, an urgent call to the vet is the most important action to take.

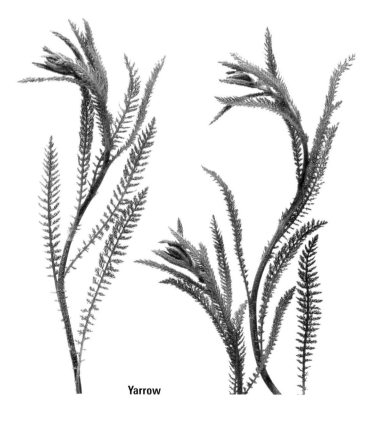

Yarrow

Homeopathy

Homeopathy can also be considered a vibrational therapy, but is treated as a medicinal therapy in this book, because it involves the administration of prepared remedies. The founder of homeopathy was Samuel Hahnemann (d.1843). He believed that every living thing has a vital life force or energy and when this energy is not balanced, illness occurs. Homeopathic remedies work on the principle that a substance that is capable of causing, in a healthy body, a similar pattern of symptoms to those being experienced, can also be used to treat that problem. The most famous example of this is that of malaria and the bark of the chinchona tree. If a healthy person takes chinchona (or quinine, the drug derived from it), he or she develops symptoms similar to those of malaria. Yet the same substance alleviates the symptoms in a person who is suffering from the disease.

About the remedies

A homeopathic remedy contains an infinitessimal amount of the natural substances from which it is derived. This is prepared through a process of "potentization" – progressive dilution and shaking (succussion). It is one of the seeming paradoxes of homeopathy that the more a remedy is diluted, the stronger its "potency." It is important to say here that the layman should not attempt to "make" homeopathic remedies. This is a highly specialized process that cannot be mimicked in a home situation. Homeopathic remedies are widely available by mail order or from health-food stores and some pharmacies and drug stores.

Finding a veterinary homeopath

The practice of homeopathy on animals has developed in parallel to its use in humans. Hahneman himself laid down some of the basic principles. There are now a number of veterinary surgeons practicing in Europe and in the US, who are also trained homeopaths and there are national and international professional homeopathic veterinary associations.

If you are interested in trying homeopathy on your horse, for best results you should try to consult an appropriately qualified person. This is because the right choice of homeopathic remedy involves much more than making a diagnosis and consulting a list of remedies. The expert will observe the animal and ask questions about his personality and behaviour before making a recommendation as to treatment. However, there are some remedies that can safely be used by a horse owner with no expert knowledge.

How to administer homeopathy

For general use, choose remedies of 6c potency. The tiny white tablets should not be touched by your hand. The best way to administer them to a horse is to tip the tablets (normally four for a horse) onto a clean, folded piece of paper and from there into the side of the horse's mouth. Remedies can be given every half-hour for acute conditions, but twice a day is more usual. A homeopathic tincture can be administered by dropping the appropriate number of drops (four times the human dose) inside the horse's mouth.

Key remedies

Apis mellifica

This is prepared from a whole bee and also from the venom diluted with alcohol. It is used where there is edema (swelling resulting from accumulation of fluid). It can also be used in conditions in which there is swelling of the synovial membranes of the joints and in allergic respiratory complaints where there is swelling of the mucous membranes.

Arnica

Arnica is the first choice homeopathic remedy for an injury, especially where there is bruising – for example, a kick from another horse.

Aconite

This is the remedy most often used in cases of shock, fright, or even panic. It can be administered after any accident or other trauma. It is also useful in the early stages of inflammatory or feverish conditions.

Belladonna

This is a remedy that anyone who has a pony who suffers from laminitis should keep in the first aid box. It can also be useful for some horses with handling difficulties.

Calcarea fluorica

Crystals of this substance are found in bone, tooth enamel, and in the outer layer of the skin (epidermis). This remedy has a particular affinity with conditions affecting the bone.

Calendula officinalis

Derived from pot marigold, this is an ideal treatment for encouraging healing of wounds, whether given in a homeopathic preparation or as the herb itself.

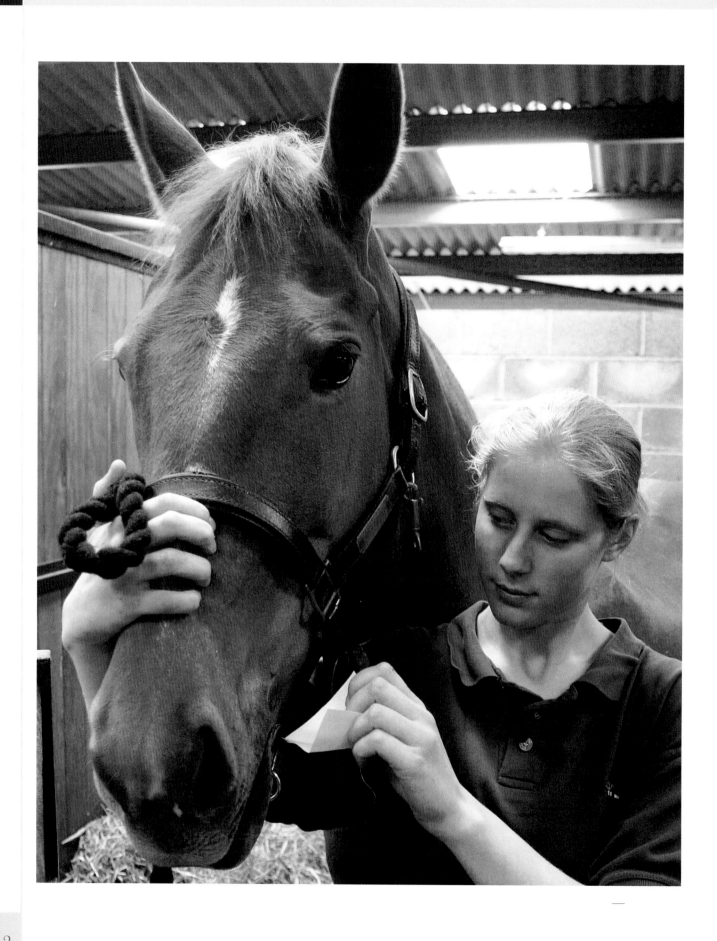

Hepar sulphuris calcareum

This remedy is used for conditions that tend to produce pus, such as respiratory infections in which there is a thick nasal discharge. It is also useful for treating suppurating wounds, especially when they are painful to touch.

Hypericum perforatum

This remedy for wounds is derived from St John's wort. It is particularly indicated in wounds in which there may be nerve damage. It can be useful to prevent proud flesh (an overgrowth of tissue when a wound heals), which can be an important consideration in show animals.

Graphites

This remedy is indicated for skin conditions in which there is a sticky, clear discharge, such sweet itch or mud fever. Graphites is often available in a cream that is effective as a topical application.

Rhus toxicodendron

This is often called the "creaking gate remedy" and is primarily used for conditions with pain and stiffness that improve after exercise. Old horses with arthritis often do well on this remedy.

Silica

This remedy is used where there is a deep wound, especially if the bone might be involved. It can also be useful to counteract poor hoof growth.

Flower essences

The best known of these are the Bach Flower Remedies. Flower essences are produced all over the world and different plants are used in different places. The basic premise is that plants and flowers can be used to heal negative states of mind that might be giving rise to physical problems in the body. Flower essences are made in different ways but mostly by soaking freshly picked flowers or other plant material in a bowl of spring water and standing in sunlight. The potentized water is then mixed with brandy to preserve it. The liquid then contains the vibrational essence of the plant (see also Vibrational healing, page 191).

Flower essences are most effective in problems that have their basis in the emotions. They are entirely safe for use in horses as in humans. Each horse has his own individual personality and for this reason may react differently

Giving a homeopathic remedy
Tip the tablets from a piece of folded paper into the horse's mouth. Since the tablets taste sweet, the horse will not normally reject them.

to a specific essence than another horse given the same remedy. A skilled practitioner will assess a horse's personality and make a recommendation for a suitable flower essence based on this assessment. In general, flower essences are administered into the side of the mouth up to four times a day, unless otherwise advised.

Key remedies

Rescue Remedy

Rescue Remedy is a combination of Impatiens, Star of Bethlehem, Cherry Plum, Rock Rose, and Clematis. It is the first remedy to use when the horse has had an accident of any kind (and is good for the rider too!). Use it also at times of emotional stress, such as when a horse arrives in a new home or has to undergo an uncomfortable procedure such as clipping. Give four drops every half hour until the crisis is over, and then two to three times a day.

Aspen

The Aspen horse is fearful of the unknown. He spooks and shies more than usual, but is confident when he knows his handler.

Administering a flower essence
Gently part your horse's lips and drop the essence into the side of his mouth.

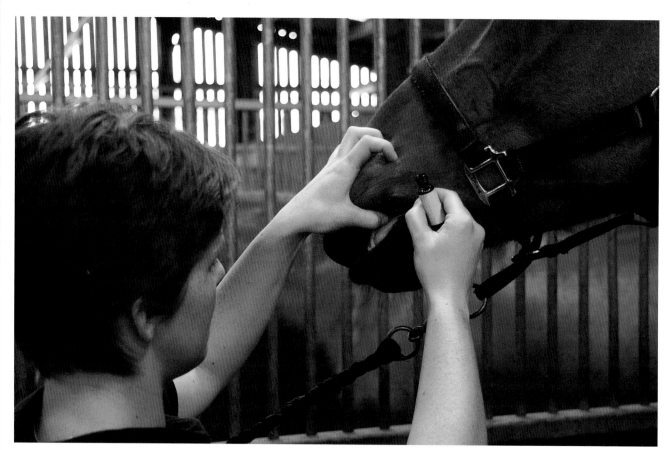

Clematis

A horse that responds poorly to training and appears dull and lethargic may benefit from this remedy.

Gorse

This remedy can help a horse that is seriously ill and that seems to have lost the will to get better.

Impatiens

Give this remedy to a horse that does not relax easily. He rushes at everything and sometimes injures himself in the process.

Oak

This flower essence is useful for raising the spirits of a horse who is confined to the stable as a result of illness or injury. It is also useful for a horse that is depressed as a result of a change of home.

Rock Rose

One of the components of Rescue Remedy, it can be used on its own to calm a horse that is frightened of fireworks or thunderstorms.

Vine

A horse that may benefit from Vine is assertive and wants to be first for everything, barging his way to the front of any group. He may also be aggressive with humans, with a tendency to bite and kick.

Hands-on therapies

Touch is a very important sense for horses as well as humans. Think about the mare touching her foal, usually laying her head over the foal's neck or body. This provides reassuring and healing contact. While just touching can contribute to your horse's well-being, trained touch applied according to a variety of different therapeutic systems can bring even greater benefits.

Physical therapy and osteopathy

Physical therapy embraces other therapies such as massage (see page 186), ultrasound treatment, and magnetic therapy. With the exception of massage, which is safe for the owner to administer, these forms of therapy must carried out by a trained expert. Osteopathy, which involves manipulation of misaligned joints, is another form of hands-on treatment that requires an expert practitioner. These therapies should always be used on the advice of your veterinary surgeon, who will recommend a practitioner.

Chiropractic

This is the favourite back treatment of many horse owners. The name means literally performed by hand. The treatment involves subtle manipulations of the body, especially the spine, where it has an effect on the nerves where they leave the spinal column. This, in turn, affects the functioning of the internal organs and the motor and sensory function of the areas of the body supplied by the nerves. The treatment consists of quick, small movements which are usually done with the hand and which, although gentle, make powerful adjustments. Sometimes a vet will recommend chiropractic treatment to resolve a specific problem. But some owners, particularly of competition horses, use chiropractic on a regular basis as a maintenance treatment even when nothing obvious is amiss.

Massage

Massage is a technique relatively easily learned by owners and, while they might not achieve the results of a professionally trained masseur, they can at least help to keep their horse's muscles more relaxed than they might otherwise have been. You can start by practicing running your hands over your horse and feeling areas where the muscles are tight. It takes a bit of time to learn to feel these areas of tension. The horse will help, by his responses. When you have, use your intuition to gently massage and rub the area. Gradually move out to the surrounding areas, massaging and stroking the muscles until they relax. This is just the beginning of massage and if you want to learn more, there are a number of very good videos around which will teach you more sophisticated techniques. A basic massage routine is described on page 73.

Shiatsu

Shiatsu massage has been well established as a form of therapy for nearly 100 years and its origins go back much further. It was developed for use in horses by Pamela Hannay in the 1980s. Shiatsu is used both as a treatment and as a form of preventative care. The word literally means finger pressure and, while this is part of the treatment, there are also a number of other

TRYING OUT AN OIL

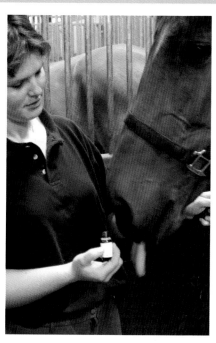

1 Hold the bottle of oil, with the lid off, near to your horse's nostril.

2 Allow him time to smell and consider the aroma.

3 Watch for signs of approval or disapproval. This horse is interested in this oil.

movements, including stroking and flat hand pressure, that are also used. The practitioner looks at the whole of the horse's life and environment and makes suggestions accordingly. Most horses seem to love shiatsu and it is well worth learning some movements from your practitioner so that you can use them to help your horse on a daily basis.

Aromatherapy

Aromatherapy is first recorded in use in Ancient Egypt at least 5,000 years ago. It was rediscovered and popularized for use on humans by the French chemist René-Maurice Gattefossé in the 1920s. This gentle therapy uses essential oils extracted from plants, which are usually either inhaled or diluted in a carrier oil and rubbed into the skin (hence its categorization here as a hands-on therapy). Never give these oils to your horse by mouth. Each oil produces a different response in the body and is therefore helpful in different conditions. Although the use of essential oils on horses is a relatively recent practice, so-called horse whisperers have traditionally rubbed lavender flowers between their hands to soothe difficult animals.

Indentifying the right oil

It is a skilled task to ascertain which oil might suit which horse, but the owner can carry out a rough-and-ready test for herself, which can often be reliable. First find out which oils might be suitable for the problem that your horse is experiencing. Then go to him with each bottle in turn and let him smell the aroma. Do be careful that he does not try to grab the bottle. If he shows interest, smelling first with one nostril and then with the other, or tries to eat the bottle, then this is the oil for him. A lack of interest means that he does not need or want that oil. If he shows a slight interest, you could offer it to him to smell again later or the next day, to try to verify the finding. This is a very crude way of assessment and if you feel that aromatherapy could really benefit your horse, you should seek advice from a veterinary aromatherapist.

Key oils

Citronella

A powerful fly repellent, this essential oil should not be applied neat to the skin, but diluted in a carrier oil.

Clary sage

Some nervous horses respond well to this oil. It also combines well with eucalyptus and frankincense for breathing difficulties such as chronic obstructive pulmonary disease (COPD).

Eucalyptus

Strongly antiseptic, this pungent oil can help to ease breathing in respiratory infections and allergies.

Frankincense

A calming oil, frankincense is primarily used to ease breathing and soothe persistent coughing as in chronic obstructive pulmonary disease (COPD).

Jasmine

This oil often helps horses with behaviour problems such as cribbing or weaving. It has also been used with success with horses that have been abused or neglected. Diluted in oil it can be used to massage the head and neck.

Lavender

A few drops of neat lavender on your hands will help to calm a horse that is nervous when handled. Lavender can be used on wounds to deter flies.

Roman chamomile

Roman chamomile can be used to alleviate itching, such as from sweet itch.

Tea tree

This oil has powerful antibacterial properties. It can be used when washing blankets and brushes to disinfect them. It is useful in mud fever and cracked heels and is added to an aloe vera based gel for application to sweet itch.

Vetiver

This oil can help steady a nervous horse or one with behaviour problems such as cribbing.

Yarrow

This oil can be used undiluted on wounds. It helps to stop bleeding and promotes healing. Yarrow added to a carrier such as almond oil makes a soothing massage oil for sprains and strains.

Cranial osteopathy

The movement of energy within the body is manifest in many ways, not least in the ebb and flow of cerebrospinal fluid that surrounds the spinal cord between the cranium and sacrum. Cranial osteopathy involves gentle manipulation of the bones of the skull to affect the movement of the cerebrospinal fluid. This subtle therapy has been adapted to horses by some practitioners. Many horses relax noticeably during treatment and beneficial effects on their health have been noted.

Zero balancing

Zero balancing has only recently been used on horses, but has been used successfully on humans since it was developed by Dr Fritz Smith, an osteopath, physician, and acupuncturist in the 1970s. It uses a system of finger pressure and "held stretches" to release deep tension from the body. There have been some very encouraging reports of horses treated by this method and whose health has been seen to improve dramatically.

Tellington Touch

The Tellington Touch Equine Awareness Method combines body work, ground work, and riding exercises to improve co-ordination, balance, and athletic ability while deepening the understanding between horse and rider. American horsewoman Linda Tellington-Jones developed this method from

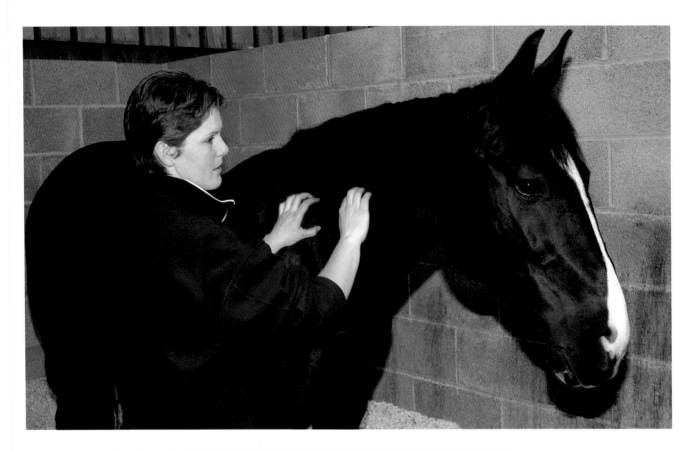

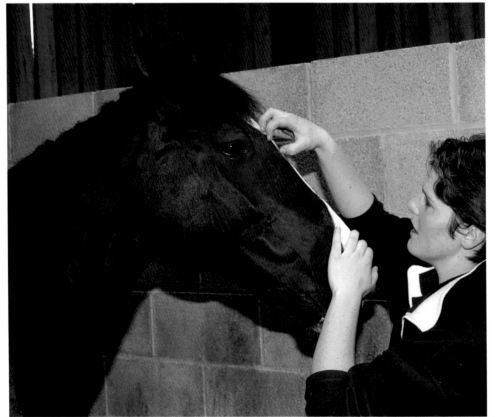

Tellington Touch – Clouded Leopard Touch

This picture shows the Clouded Leopard Touch which is the basic touch for all over the horse's body. The hand is held open like a cat's paw and the the tips of the fingers are used to apply gentle pressure in tiny circular movements

Tellington Touch – Racoon Touch

In the Racoon Touch the fingers are held closer together. The touch is performed lightly with the tips of the fingers (but not the nails) and is used on more sensitive areas, such as the face.

the Feldenkrais method of awareness through movement. The posture of the horse affects some of its behaviours and encouraging the horse to change its posture and leave its instinctive responses behind can improve its behaviour and make riding much more enjoyable. By looking at your horse you may be able to judge its temperament from its posture. For example, a horse with a tightly clamped tail, does not like movement or noise behind him. Because of the tension in his hindquarters, he will not go forward properly when ridden and will not find jumping easy. By using the exercises in this method, the horse should gradually release the tension held in his tail and hindquarters and will therefore be easier and safer to ride. There are a number of books and videos available on this method, and there are regular demonstrations in UK and USA.

Vibrational healing

Vibrational healing is a general description of therapies that draw on the idea that that every living thing has an energy force that affects its well-being. This energy, although invisible is vital to survival and can be affected by other vibrations such as those emitted naturally by such phenomena as light, sound, colour, magnets, plants, crystals, and other beings.

Many alternative therapies that have been dealt with separately in this section also make use of these ideas. The therapies detailed below are fast finding credence in the horse world, as horse owners and keepers begin to realize that horses as well as humans can benefit from a therapy which puts their life force back on the right track and therefore helps the body to heal itself. It is thought that modern day living causes human beings to have unbalanced energy systems. Surely modern day living for horses must have this effect too?

Acupuncture

Acupuncture is one of the oldest forms of treatment. It originated in China at least 3,000 years ago. Whether in horses or in humans, in Chinese medicine the body is regarded as a whole and any problem is seen as a manifestation of imbalance in the system. According to traditional Chinese medicine, energy or *qi* (pronounced chee) flows through a system of channels or meridians. It must be flowing freely along the meridians for good health to be maintained. Disease manifests as a disturbance in the *qi*, or as an interruption in the smooth and regular flow of *qi* in the meridians. Acupuncture aims to influence the free flow of *qi* by inserting fine needles at certain points along the meridians. Once the energy is balanced and flowing freely, according to Chinese medicine, the body will be able to start healing itself. The insertion of needles alone is unlikely to produce sustained healing: dietary measures, lifestyle changes, and, sometimes herbal treatments are often recommended for best results. In some cases, an acupuncturist will add to the effect by running a low voltage electrical current through the needles.

Physiological effects

Scientific tests in humans have shown that placing needles in certain points on the body can cause the body to release various chemicals that are known to have pain-relieving properties. These endorphins and enkephalins have similar actions to those of narcotic drugs. No doubt this is also why

Inserting the needle
Acupuncture needles are so fine that in most cases the horse seems hardly to notice when they are inserted.

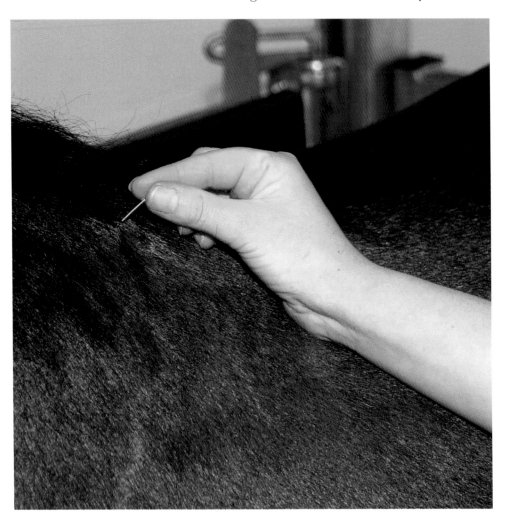

acupuncture can be so effective in controlling pain in animals. It may also explain the effectiveness of the twitch. This is a twisted loop of rope attached to a short stick, which is wound tightly around the upper lip. When properly used, it will instantly cause the horse to stand calmly while he is being clipped or undergoing other uncomfortable procedures. Its effects may be in part due to the fact that when correctly applied it exerts pressure over a powerful acupuncture point. A twitch should only be used by someone who has been taught to do so properly. It can cause severe pain to your horse if incorrectly applied because of the sensitivity of the nose and muzzle.

Like many alternative therapies, with proper supervision, acupuncture can be combined with other alternative and orthodox treatments. In fact, this form of treatment is not often used in isolation. In many countries, including the USA and UK, acupuncture may only be practiced legally by qualified veterinary surgeons.

Perhaps surprisingly, most horses seem to enjoy this therapy, relaxing, yawning, resting a leg and showing other signs of being at peace while the treatment is carried out. A minority of horses, however, do object and become restless or agitated when the needles are inserted. In such cases it may be best to use another form of treatment. There are usually no side effects to acupuncture treatment.

When acupuncture is most useful

A wide variety of conditions respond well to acupuncture. Most painful conditions can be relieved by this treatment, with the caveat that the underlying cause of the pain must, of course, also be addressed. Acupuncture can also be effective for muscle injuries (where it promotes healing) and in inflammatory pain of longstanding, such as arthritis.

Allergic conditions such COPD (see page 149) may respond to acupuncture especially in the acute stages. A disorder of this kind will not be cured by acupuncture and will not indeed by relieved until the appropriate measures have been taken to separate the horse from the allergen. However, when breathing is acutely difficult, acupuncture can rapidly help to restore the breathing to normal. Other allergies, such as sweet itch (see page 153), can often be effectively relieved by combining acupuncture with herbal treatments and topical applications as appropriate. Various other conditions ranging from infertility to stress may also benefit from acupuncture.

Amethyst

Citrine

Quartz

Moonstone

Crystal healing

Crystals are naturally formed rocks or stones, with the most precious varieties being gemstones. Crystals vibrate on slightly different frequencies, depending on their type, where they came from and how they have been handled in the interim. Experts in crystal healing believe that human and animal health can benefit from the healing effect of crystal vibrations.

It is important when choosing crystals for your horse that you hold the crystal in your hand and think strongly about your horse. In most cases you will get a sense as to whether this is the right crystal for him or not. It is important that crystals are regularly recharged and cleansed. This can be done simply under a running tap while you visualize natural running water or by leaving them in sunlight for 24 hours.

Key crystals

Quartz or rock crystal

This crystal balances and clears. For a sick horse sew pointed oblong pieces of quartz into his blanket or tie them onto his halter (headcollar).

Amethyst

This is calming and cleansing. It combats negativity and pollution. Use as for quartz and rock crystal.

Citrine

Dispels fears and can be useful for nervous horses. Attach a small piece to the bridle of a nervous horse.

Moonstone

Ideal for mares with hormonal problems. A piece in the stable will help her to settle down.

Sound therapy

Many horses appear to love music. Many stables and barns have a radio playing as company for the horses. Their behaviour will be affected by the type of music being played. Pachabel's Canon in D is a very well known piece of music, which when played to people recovering from general anesthesia has been shown to speed their return to consciousness. This same piece of music when played to horses seems to have a calming effect. If you have a highly strung horse, experiment with different types of music and even with some of the New Age compilations that include natural sounds such as the sounds of the sea or a river, and see how your horse responds. A horse that was an inveterate wind-sucker stopped wind-sucking altogether to listen to Gregorian chant!

Light and colour therapy

The healing power of sunlight for horses is often greatly underestimated. The delicate balance of wavelengths that occurs in sunlight is vital for most living things. Horses that are deprived of sunlight fail to thrive in the same way that many humans who suffer the same deprivation may become ill. It is thought that sunlight has a particularly strong effect on hormone levels. Many mares, especially ponies, come into season as soon as they feel the first spring sunlight on their backs. This is Nature's way of ensuring that the foal

Growing in the sun
A foal needs plenty of natural light if he is to thrive. Mares and foals should spend a high proportion of their time out of doors.

is born in warm weather. The foal then benefits from plentiful sunlight to ensure optimal development. In addition, exposure to light and air promotes the healing of wounds and keeps infection at bay.

In long dark winters, horses – especially those who do not spend much time turned out – can benefit from sessions with a properly designed full-spectrum lamp. In the 1920s Dr John Ott found that animals kept under full-spectrum light always produced more and healthier young than those exposed to other kinds of lighting. Brood mares therefore should be kept outside, unless there are overriding reasons why this is not possible.

Horses are thought to have a relatively poor appreciation of colour, so painting his stable a different colour to affect his mood may not work. However, if you are having difficulty in your relationship with your horse, then wearing an appropriate colour yourself may help you to cope with the problem and your horse will be the beneficiary. Green is said to balance the mind and heal the body. Pink is warming soothing and reassuring. Yellow represents patience, tolerance, and wisdom.

Magnet therapy

Many horse owners wear a magnet on their wrist to help with their minor aches and pains and increasingly magnet boots, blankets, collars, and other devices are becoming available for horses. When the magnet is placed next to the body, it appears to increase the flow of blood to the area, but also to a lesser degree generally, and therefore to stimulate healing. Magnet therapy is most often used to alleviate minor strains and stiffness in horses. It may also speed wound healing. However, take care not to use magnets directly over the site of a recent open wound as this may increase bleeding.

Spiritual healing

This above all others is the area of vibrational healing that produces the most "miracle cures" and conversely attracts the most charlatans. There are no instruments and no drugs. Sometimes the healer does not even touch the horse. The healer claims to be a channel through which the healing energy can flow. He or she can sense disturbances in this flow within the animal, and can direct the healing energy accordingly. There are no qualifications for this type of healing: when selecting a practitioner you have to rely on evidence from other horses that have been successfully treated and your own common sense and judgment.

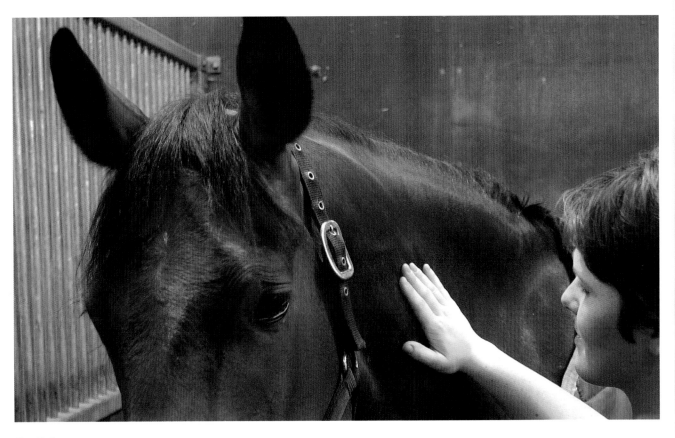

Reiki

The word Reiki means universal life energy. It involves the channeling of this universal energy, through a person, who is the giver, to the patient. The giver is also simultaneously healed and re-energized. Reiki is often the basis of other forms of healing, such as laying on hands, and other techniques such as horse whispering.

Reiki is carried out by laying the hands on the horse's body and head. For example, you might start by laying your hands on his forehead and then slowly moving your hands to each side of his face. You could then move your hands to the horse's body. However, there are no set guidelines as to where to touch or in what order, but if you relax yourself and let your hands move naturally, you will usually find the right place.

Many horses respond positively to Reiki contact, and it can be particularly beneficial for a horse that is confused and stressed by life in general. For example, it can be used on a horse to settle him in new surroundings or to calm him after an accident. Anyone can study to be a Reiki giver and many short courses are available.

Healing hands
The calming touch of your hands when applied with conscious healing intent can have a powerful effect on promoting well-being.

Further Reading

Allison, Keith. *A Guide to Alternative Therapies for Horses.* J.A. Allen, 1996.

Allison, Keith. *The Holistic Management of Horses.* J.A. Allen, 1996.

Daniel, Dr. Kamen. *The Well Adjusted Horse: Equine Chiropractic Methods You Can Do.* Brookline Books, 1999.

Hannay, Pamela and Kaselle, Marion. *Touching Horses.* J.A. Allen, 1995.

Howard, Judy. *The Bach Flower Remedies Step-by-Step.* C.W. Daniel, 1990.

Ingraham, Caroline. *Aromatherapy for Horses.* Kenilworth Press, 1997.

Kiley-Worthington, Dr Marthe. *The Behaviour of Horses.* J.A. Allen, 1987.

Macleod, George. *The Treatment of Horses by Homoeopathy.* C.W. Daniel, 1997.

Morgan, Jenny. *Herbs for Horses.* Kenilworth Press, 1994.

Page Self, Hilary. *A Modern Horse Herbal.* Kenilworth Press, 1996.

Townley, Audrey. *The Natural Horse.* Crowood Press, 1993.

Wanless, Mary. *For the Good of The Horse.* Kenilworth Press, 1997.

Wanless, Mary. *Ride With Your Mind.* Kenilworth Press, 1987.

Wyche, Sara. *The Horse Owner's Guide to Holistic Medicine.* Crowood Press, 1996.

Zidonis, Nancy A. and Snow, Amy. *Equine Acupressure: A Working Manual.* Equine Acupressure Inc., 1999.

Useful Addresses

UK

Organizations

Association of Chartered Physiotherapists in
Animal Therapy
c/o Mrs. Joyce Verey
Morland House
Salters Lane
Winchester
Hants SO22 5JP
Tel. 01962 844390
email secretary@acpat.org.uk

British Association of Homeopathic Veterinary
Surgeons
Chinham House
Stanford in the Vale
Oxon SN7 8NQ
Tel. 01367 710324
www.bahvs.com

British Horse Society
Stoneleigh Deer Park
Kenilworth
Warwickshire CV8 2XZ
Tel. 08701 202 244
Fax 01926 707 800
www.bhs.org.uk

Dr Edward Bach Centre
Mount Vernon
Sotwell
Wallingford
Oxon OX10 OPZ

The Farriers Registration Council
Sefton House
Adam Court
Newark Road
Peterborough PE1 5PP
Tel. 01733 319911
Fax 01733 319910

International Federation for Vibrational Medicine
Middle Piccadilly Healing Centre
Holwell
Sherborne
Dorset DT9 5LW
Tel. 01963 23468

McTimoney College of Chiropractic
The Clock House
22-26 Ock Street
Abingdon OX14 5SH
Tel. 01235 523336
Fax 01235 523576
www.mctimoney-college.ac.uk

Ponies Association (UK)
Chesham House
56 Green End Road
Sawtry
Huntingdon PE28 5UY
Tel. 08700 785 123
Fax 01487 832086
email info@poniesuk.org
www.poniesuk.org

The Pony Club
Stoneleigh Deer Park
Kenilworth
Warwickshire CV8 2RW
Tel. 024 7669 8300
Fax 024 7669 6836
www.pony-club.co.uk

Radionics and Radiesthesia Trust
Maperton
Wincanton
Somerset BA9 8EH
Tel. 01963 32651

Tellington Touch Equine Awareness
Sunnyside House
Stratton Audley Road
Fringford
Oxon OX6 9ED
Tel. 01869 277730

Zero Balancing for Horses
www.zerobalancing.com

Suppliers

Ainsworths Homeopathic Pharmacy
36 New Cavendish Street
London W1M 7LH
Tel. 020 7935 5330
www.ainsworths.com

Anaflora Flower Essences for Animals
www.anaflora.com

Bayhouse Aromatics
St George's Road
Brighton
West Sussex BN2 1EE
Tel. 01273 601109

Earthstar Animal Healing
Almadel Natural Health
19 Newbury Cottages
Coleford
Bath BA3 5RU
Tel. 01373 812864

East West Herbs Ltd.
Langston Priory Mews
Kingham
Oxon OX7 6UP
Tel. 01608 658862

Equine Shiatsu (Cathy Tindall)
Otley Farm
Haversham
Milton Keynes MK19 7DN.
Tel. 01908 316122
www.cathytindall.com

Hilton Herbs Ltd.
Downclose Farm
North Perrot
Crewkerne
Somerset TA18 7SH
Tel. 01460 78300

Horse Directory
www.horse-directory.co.uk

Intelligent Horsemanship (Kelly Marks)
Lethornes
Lambourn
Hungerford
Berks RG17 8QS
Tel. 01488 71300

Magno-Pulse Ltd.,
Leabrook Lodge
Lower Strode Road
Bristol BS21 6UU
Tel. 01275 874615

Natural Animal Feeds
Penrhos
Raglan
Monmouthshire NP15 2DJ
Tel. 01600 780 256

Natural Animal Health
www.natural-animal-health.co.uk
Nelson and Co Ltd.
(Homeopathic pharmacy/mail order)
Broadheath House
83 Parkside
London SW19 5LP
Tel. 020 8780 4200

Ride With Your Mind (Mary Wanless)
Overdale Equestrian Centre
Nether Westcote
Nr Chipping Norton
Oxon OX7 6SD
Tel. 01993 831193

USA

Organizations

American Association of Horsemanship Safety
Drawer 39
Fentress, TX 78622
Tel. 512-488-2220

American Holistic Veterinary Medical Association
2218 Old Emmorton Road
Bel Air
Maryland 21015
Tel. 410-569-0795
Fax 410-569-2346
email: AHVMA@compuserve.com

American Horse Council
1700 K Street NW, Suite 300
Washington DC 20006
Tel. 202-296-4031
Fax 202-296-1970
www.horsecouncil.org

Horsemanship Safety Association
517 Bear Road
Lake Placid, FL 33852
Tel. 800-798-8106

USEFUL ADDRESSES

National 4-H Council
7100 Connecticut Avenue
Chevy Chase, MD 20815-4999
Tel. 301-961-2937
www.4-H.org

National FFA Organization
P.O. Box 68960
6060 FFA Drive
Indianapolis, IN 46268
Tel. 317-802-6060/1

U.S. Pony Clubs, Inc.
The Kentucky Horse Park
4041 Iron Works Parkway
Lexington, KY 40511-8462
Tel. 859-254-7669
www.ponyclub.org

U.S.A. Equestrian (formerly American Horse
Shows Association (AHSA)
4047 Iron Works Parkway
Lexington, KY 40511-8483
Tel. 859-258-2472
www.equestrian.org

Magazines

Equine Journal
103 Roxbury St.
Keene, NH 03431
Tel. 603-357-4271
www.equinejournal.com

Equus
656 Quince Orchard Road
Suite 600
Gaithersburg, MD 20878
Tel. 800-829-5910
Equus@Palmcoastd.com

Natural Horse Magazine
P.O. Box 10
Holtwood, PA 17532
Tel. 800-660-8923
email publisher@naturalhorse.com
www.naturalhorse.com

202

Index

Numbers in *italics* refer to captions to illustrations.

abortion 147, 166
accidents 144
acorns 47
acupuncture 123, 124, 191, 192, *192*, 193
adrenal gland 162
Aesculus hippocastanum 47
aggression 102, *102*, 103
alfalfa 52
allergies
  acupuncture 193
  bedding 42
  COPD 149, 150
  dust 40
  laminitis 132
  skin 150, 151
  sweet itch 153
Allium sativum 175
Allium ursinum 176
aloe vera 189
American Standardbred 16
amethyst 194, *194*
amniotic sac 165
anemia 145
aniseed 148
anthrax 161
antibiotics 172
  feeding 54
  horse care 17
  mud fever 155
  thrush 142
antihistamine 176
antimonium tartaricum 148
antiseptic cream 120
Apis mellifica 181
appetite loss 159
apple cider vinegar 131, 154
apples 52, 121
Arab horses 15, 29, 32
Arab-type horses 14
arena work 69, 88, 92
Arnica 181
aromatherapy 187
arthritis 130, *130*

herbal medicine 173
Aspen 184
Atropa belladonna 47
automatic waterers 55
azoturia 162

Bach Flower Remedies 183
back,
  balance 86
  cold 106, 107
  healthy horse 25
  natural riding 76
  stretching *71*
bad behaviour 98, 99
balance,
  feet 62, 63
  riding 86, *86*, 88, 92, 93
  spine 76
balking 106, 107
bandages 120, 122, 123
barley 52
barn stabling system 39, 40, 41, *42*, 43
bedding 40, 42, 43, 44
  COPD 149, *149*
  sick horse 119, *119*
beech, beechmast 47
behaviour,
  equine stereotype 108
  ill health 115
  learned 13
  natural 18, 38
  problems 96, 97, *97*, 98, 99
  stabling 41
Belladonna 181
berries, poisonous 47
bicarbonate of soda 159
birth 165, 166
bites,
  insect 151, 177
  lice 152
  sweet itch 153
biting 99, 102, *102*
bitless bridle 85
bits 82, 83, *83*, 84
blackberries 48
blankets 48, 49, 50
  Western saddles 82
bleeding 116, 118

foot 30
  signs of ill health 115
  wounds 156
blood pressure 176
blowing 61, 65, 70
body brush 56
bog spavin 139
bolting 35
bone spavin 139
bosal bridle *85*
bowel inflammation 146
boxes, stabling *39*, 40, 41, 47, *101*
box-walking 99, 108
bracken 47
brambles 48
bran 52
breastplate 81
breathing, 27, 62
  emergency 116
  fitness 61, 65, 70
  healthy horse 25
  relaxation 72
  riding 92
breathing difficulties,
  signs of ill health 115
breeding,
  behaviour 96
  reproduction 163
breeds 14, 15
brewer's grains 52
bridle 82, 83, 84
  English *83*
  fitting *84*
  Western *85*
broken limbs 116
broken wind 149
brood mares 196
browband 84
Brucella abortus 161
brucellosis 161
bruising 141, 156
brushes 56, 57
Bryonia 162, 148
bucking 90, 106, 107, *107*
buttercups 47
Buxus sempervirens 47
buying 33, *34*, 35, 38

Calcarea fluorica 181
calcium 53, 138, 146

calendula 177
Calendula officinalis 177
Calendula officinalis 181
Camargue horses 17, *51*
cancers 160, 161, 162
canine teeth 160
cannon bone *71*, 137
cantering 30, 65, 96
cantle 77
cardboard bedding 42
carpitis 130
carrots 52, 121
cart horses 140
cartilage 130, 138
catching 98, 99, 100, *100*
cavalry horses 52
center of balance 78
Centered Riding 88
cereals 52, 53
chaff 52
chamomile 179
  Roman 189
cheek pieces,
  bits 83
  bosal bridle 85
  English bridle *83*, *84*
  Western bridle *85*
Cherry plum 184
chestnut horses 176
chili oil 131
chiropractic treatment 65, 110, 124, 186
choking 52
chronic obstructive pulmonary disease (COPD) 149, *149*
cinch 62, *80*, *81*, 82
citrine 194, *194*
Citronella 150, 188
Clary sage 188
cleansing agents 120
cleavers 134
Clematis 184, 185
clenches 30
clipping 48, 60, 64
clothing, riding 90
coat 48
  clipping 64, 65
  conditioner 176
  examination 29
  grooming 55, *56*

healthy horse 24
  problems 150
  signs of ill health 115
cold back 106, 107
cold pack 120
colic 144, 145
  digestive disorders 142, 143
  emergency 116
  grass 121
  intestinal parasites 145
  signs of ill health 115
colon *143*
colour therapy 191, 195, 196
coltishness 163
coltsfoot 148
compound feed 18, 52, 53, 146
conformation 64, 76
Conium maculatum 47
conjunctivitis 159
cooler sheet *49*, 70
cooling down 70, *70*
corns 141
coronet band 30
cotton blankets *49*
cough,
  COPD 149
  respiratory disease 148
  signs of ill health 115, 121
cowboy 17, 81
cracked heel 154, 189
cranial osteopathy 189
crest 29
cribbing 35, 99, 108, *108*
cross-country 78
crystal healing 194
curb bit 85, *85*
curry comb *56*
Cushing's disease 162, 176
cuts 55

daffodil 47
dandelion 48, 175, *175*
dandy brush 56
deadly nightshade 47

Acknowledgments

Gaia Books would like to thank the following for their help in the preparation of this book:
Philip Cheetham and Sarah Phillips of Hartpury College, and Chris Brodie, Lizzie Brooks, Amy Porter, Catherine Porter, Rosie Scott, Paula Williams, Sam Williams, who modeled for the photographs.
Joan Johnston and Hayley, Barnet Riding Centre.
Derek Williams.

Photographic credits
Unless otherwise stated all photographs are by Vincent Oliver.
Bob Langrish: 2, 5, 6, 10, 13, 14, 15, 16, 18, 19, 20, 31, 36, 39, 40, 42, 43, 44, 46, 51, 53, 58, 61, 64, 66, 68 (bottom), 69, 70, 94, 97, 98 (right), 102, 103 (bottom), 104, 105, 106, 107, 109, 111, 112, 126, 130, 131, 144, 152, 154, 155, 157, 162, 165, 169, 170.
Philip Dowell: 175, 177, 178.
Adrian Swift: 194.

Other Storey Titles You Will Enjoy

Getting Your First Horse *by Judith Dutson.*
Everything a new or prospective horse owner needs to know about selecting a horse, the needs of a horse, terminology, horse-handling techniques, and more.
176 pages. Paperback. ISBN 1-58017-078-1

Horse Handling and Grooming *by Cherry Hill.*
A user-friendly guide, complete with 350 how-to-photographs, presenting correct techniques for leading, haltering, typing, grooming, clipping, bathing, braiding, hoof handling, and more.
160 pages. Paperback. ISBN 0-88266-956-7.

Horse Health Care *by Cherry Hill.*
Practical advice, complete with 350 how-to photographs, on dozens of essential skills, including daily examination, restraint, leg wrapping, hoof care, administering shots, dental care, wound care, and more.
160 pages. Paperback. ISBN 0-88266-955-9

Horsekeeping on a Small Acreage: Facilities Design and Management *by Cherry Hill.*
How to design safe and functional facilities for your horse.
192 pages. Paperback. ISBN 0-88266-596-0

Horse Sense *by John J. Mettler, Jr. D.V.M.*
Advice from a country veterinarian on preventive health care, breeding, foaling, feeding, and more.
160 pages. Paperback. ISBN 0-88266-545-6

Stablekeeping *by Cherry Hill.*
A photographic guide to providing a safe, healthy, and efficient environment for a horse. Includes information on stalls, tack rooms, work and storage areas, sanitation and pest control, feeding practices, safety and emergencies, and more.
160 pages. Paperback

Storey's Guide to Raising Horses *by Heather Smith Thomas.*
The complete reference for the horse owner with detailed coverage of feeding and nutrition, foot care, disease prevention, dental care, breeding, foaling, and caring for the young horse.
512 pages. Paperback. ISBN 1-58017-127-3

Storey's Horse-Lover's Encyclopedia *edited by Deborah Burns.*
An illustrated, English & Western A-to-Z guide to healthy horse care, breeds, terminology, and lore.
476 pages. Paperback. ISBN 1-58017-317-9

Trailering Your Horse *by Cherry Hill.*
A photographic guide to low-stress traveling, including selecting a trailer, training, loading, packing, safe driving, and care en route.
160 pages. Paperback. ISBN 1-58017-176-1